# RECOVERY
## FROM
# DIVORCE

# RECOVERY FROM DIVORCE

### with
### Study Guide

### Bob Burns

## THOMAS NELSON PUBLISHERS
### Nashville

Published in Nashville, Tennessee, by Oliver-Nelson books, a
division of Thomas Nelson, Inc., Publishers, and distributed in
Canada by Lawson Falle, Ltd., Cambridge, Ontario. Originally
titled *Through the Whirlwind*.

Unless otherwise noted, the Bible version used in this
publication is THE NEW KING JAMES VERSION. Copyright
© 1979, 1980, 1982, Thomas Nelson, Inc., Publishers.

Scripture quotations noted PHILLIPS are from J. B. Phillips: THE
NEW TESTAMENT IN MODERN ENGLISH, Revised Edition.
© J. B. Phillips 1958, 1960, 1972. Used by permission of
Macmillan Publishing Co., Inc.

Scripture quotations marked TLB are from *The Living Bible*,
copyright 1971 by Tyndale House Publishers, Wheaton, IL. Used
by permission.

Scripture quotations marked NIV are from the HOLY BIBLE:
NEW INTERNATIONAL VERSION. Copyright © 1973, 1978,
1984 by the International Bible Society. Used by permission of
Zondervan Bible Publishers.

**Library of Congress Cataloging-in-Publication Data**

Burns, Bob, 1950-
    Recovery from divorce : with study guide / Bob Burns.
      p.  cm.
    Reprint of the author's Through the whirlwind, with the
addition of a study guide.
    ISBN 0-8407-9149-6
    1. Divorced people—Religious life.  2. Divorce—Religious
aspects—Christianity.  3. Divorced people—Pastoral
counseling of.
I. Burns, Bob, 1950-    Through the whirlwind.  1992.  II.
Title.
BV4596.D58B87   1993
248.8'46—dc20                            92–33819
                                          CIP

Printed in the United States of America.
2 3 4 5 6 7 8 9 10 - 97 96 95 94 93

# CONTENTS

# PREFACE

It was a hot, sticky summer day in Philadelphia. A number of friends were helping me reinsulate our home. I had torn out all of the walls on the second story. The place was a mess! We had drywall dust mingled with the heavy perspiration streaming from our bodies.

The phone rang. Someone else picked it up and called out to me: "Long-distance call from Janet."

My wife was pregnant, and I had encouraged her to get out of the house while the worst of the repairs was taking place. She had gone to Washington, D.C. to visit her mother and my brother and sister-in-law.

When I picked up the phone, I instantly sensed that something was wrong. Janet was calling from the emergency room of the local hospital. Her water had broken. The baby was to be born premature. I needed to come immediately.

This wasn't our first crisis pregnancy. Our son Trooper had also been born premature. All kinds

of fears began to swirl around my heart and mind
as I quickly threw some clothes together for the
trip.

Jeff, one of the guys working at my house, knew
that I wasn't in any condition to travel on my own.
He jumped into his car and drove me all the way to
the hospital in Virginia. During the trip, we talked
about everything except what I was about to face.

When I arrived at the hospital, the prognosis
wasn't good. The baby was in distress, and they
were about to take my wife into the delivery room.
A short time later our second son was born. However, he did not survive the trauma. He was dead.
And with his death we began the natural grief response to a crisis.

There is no way we can live in this world and
avoid crisis experiences. Injury, death, and disappointment confront us. Somewhere in the recesses
of our minds there is the conviction that things
ought to be better. We feel that somehow we deserve to be happy. However, the longer we live, the
more we realize how unrealistic it is for us to expect continuous happiness and to avoid problems.

The experience my wife and I faced in the death
of our son took us on a roller coaster of emotions.
Over the next weeks and months we drew on all of
our resources to cope. Some days went well, but
others were the pits.

We knew our grief and pain were not unique. We
were sharing in the worldwide fellowship of suffering. Suffering and grief take many forms in re-

sponse to a crisis situation. Yet for the individual involved, his particular grief is as significant as the pain brought about by any other type of crisis. For example, try telling a woman who has miscarried a child early in pregnancy that her grief has less significance than, say, the death of a spouse in the prime of life. To the one suffering, such comparisons are irrational and insensitive.

Divorce is a crisis experience. It is a crisis as significant and as personal as death. In a very real way it represents a death: the death of a relationship. The grief and the restructuring of life associated with divorce have common characteristics shared with all crisis experiences. However, some characteristics make divorce unique unto itself. These unique aspects of the divorce experience are what we seek to understand.

This book focuses on the personal side of divorce. My primary purpose is to explore the emotional transition from divorce to recovery. This limited purpose has forced me to exclude a great deal of information as well as to refrain from commenting on many critical concerns related to divorce. However, this is only the first of a projected series of books covering a full range of topics on separation, divorce, and other related matters prepared by the staff associates of Fresh Start Seminars, Inc.

The Fresh Start program began in 1980 when a group of individuals from Church of the Saviour in Wayne, Pennsylvania, felt burdened to explore ways to help persons who have suffered marital breakdown and its stresses. Over the next several years we developed Fresh Start, which has quickly spread to many locations throughout the United States.

Although the familiar *I* is used throughout the book, actually three of us have been involved in its development. Bob Burns has been the lead author, with suggestions, editorial corrections and support coming from Tom Whiteman and Tom Jones. Each individual is part of the research and speaking team of Fresh Start Seminars.

Since its inception, Fresh Start Seminars, Inc., has been designed to provide resources, seminars, and consultation on divorce-related issues to churches and professional health and social service agencies. Workshops and seminars developed by Fresh Start cover areas such as divorce recovery, life as a single-again adult, blended families, dysfunctional families, kids in the middle, adult children of divorce, and single sexuality. For further information on ways Fresh Start could help your church or organization, contact Fresh Start Seminars, Inc., 651 North Wayne Avenue, Wayne, PA 19087.

Because the English language does not contain a one-word equivalent for "he-or-she," I have generally referred to another person as "he." It would impede communication to repeatedly state "he or she."

As the lead author, I would like to share a special word of appreciation for my wife, Janet, and two sons, Trooper and Christopher. Their support and commitment to me, to Fresh Start, and to the development of this book has been invaluable. Also a special word of thanks goes to Paul and Phyllis Malone, who have poured out their lives for single-again adults and for Fresh Start. Words cannot express the depth of appreciation hundreds feel for their ministry.

# INTRODUCTION

I have to chuckle every time I remember that bumper sticker. The exact wording is lost, but the phrase went something like this:

TOTO, I DON'T THINK WE ARE
IN KANSAS ANY LONGER.

Almost everyone can pinpoint where this phrase comes from, *The Wizard of Oz.* But why is it so appropriate for the bumper sticker of a late model pickup in the middle of a busy intersection?

It is appropriate because we understand how Dorothy felt! Caught up in a whirlwind, she found herself in a new and unforeseen crisis situation. How "normal" life had been before the whirlwind. How strange, new, and different things were now.

Sometimes, when we are in a crisis situation such as separation or divorce, we feel like Dorothy: disoriented and afraid. We don't know where we are or how we got there. After all, no one originally planned to get a divorce.

Yet divorces do happen. Many of you reading this book know this from firsthand experience. Therefore, the purpose of this book is to help you make your divorce experience an occasion for growth rather than one of prolonged emotional crippling.

Where are you in the divorce process? Perhaps you are only contemplating separation. Maybe you are in the thick of litigation. Or you might have gone through divorce years ago. At whatever point you find yourself, you need to review how you got there. Then you can move toward where you want to be in the present and the future. This book is designed to guide you in reviewing the past, understanding the present, and planning for the future.

Let me briefly outline the progression of the book so you can get an idea of where we will be heading. The first four chapters present divorce from a perspective broader than the confines of your personal experience. Chapter 1 explains that divorce is a crisis experience every bit as traumatic as death. Chapter 2 prepares you to understand the emotional dynamics of divorce by reviewing the bonding that takes place when two people marry. The third and fourth chapters examine that difficult time preceding the divorce decision and the impact of that decision on both you and your family.

Chapters 5 through 9 look at the *slippery slope*— a model of the emotional stages that occur during the grief process—in detail. Finally, chapter 10 points to the resources that God has made available to those who are facing the challenge of divorce.

At the end of the book there are two appendixes written in response to questions that some people have asked concerning the topic of divorce recovery. First, many well-meaning people have said, "Are we really responsible to care for the needs of the divorced?" In Appendix A I address this question.

Second, another question has stemmed from the use of the emotional stages model. "Is this model appropriate?" some have wondered. Appendix B deals with this issue.

The stories that you will read on the following pages are true or are based on composite experiences. Names and other details have been changed in order to disguise each person to protect his or her privacy.

My desire is that you reach a better understanding of your divorce experience and think through what you can do to recover from it. This is not a how-to book, for each divorce involves a unique set of experiences and circumstances. However, ideas and steps will be suggested that many persons have found helpful as they work toward personal recovery and wholeness. I want to encourage and support you as you move through the whirlwind and become reoriented into the mainstream of life as a single-again adult.

# CHAPTER ONE

# What Am I Going Through?

Peter grew up in a typical middle American home. His parents were conscientious Christians who raised their children to respect and love both their family and their church. Upon graduation from high school Peter went to Bible college with the goal of entering the ministry. After his third year in college, he married his high-school sweetheart. Together they planned to build a family and ministry based on the principles of Peter's parents. And they confidently expected God's blessing.

Sound too good to be true? Well, it was! After two years of marriage, Peter's wife decided that she was going to pursue a new life direction—without her husband. Suddenly all of the plans, expectations, and goals of Peter's life fell apart.

Peter tells the story in his own words: "My life was all set. Then I had to start over. Everything I counted on was lost: my vocational life, my married life, my home, and my friends. Even my fam-

ily rejected me in their confusion over the divorce.
I felt like my life was over and I was powerless to
undo the damage."

## A Crisis Experience

Peter's separation and divorce sent him into the
whirlwind of a crisis experience. When we hear
the word *crisis* we usually think in terms of the
crash of an airliner, a nuclear plant disaster, or a
major epidemic. And each of these things could be
classified as a crisis.

But a crisis experience does not have to be a national catastrophe. It is usually not so dramatic,
although it can be just as frightening. It can be like
flying in an airplane and hitting an air pocket. A
sudden disruption seems to knock everything
around. The steady state of life is disrupted.

Of course, a personal crisis can come in the
form of a sudden, unexpected event, such as an au-
tomobile accident or the diagnosis of cancer.
When the shock hits, it seems as though the whole
world closes down around that one set of circumstances.

However, a crisis can also develop out of a pro-
tracted condition. I think of a couple I heard about
recently who spent years in an off and on separation. They always talked about the problems keeping them apart. But they never did anything about

these problems. They lived in a constant ebb and flow of crisis.

Or consider when a business failure drains the family of financial strength and saps the emotional investment of the partners. They face the long-standing crisis of living in continual financial uncertainty and marital instability.

Whatever the reason, a crisis can occur when one's steady state of life is shaken. It can affect all aspects of one's life, including the primary relationships providing one's support system.

Glenn experienced a significant crisis that drastically altered his life. It took place on a beautiful Saturday in August. He had volunteered to assist the senior-high ministry of his church as they took busloads of kids to the beach. Glenn had gone on many trips like this in the past. He knew the high-school gang and was looking forward to spending a great day with them.

Glenn's crisis occurred late in the afternoon. Some of the guys began to kid around with him, and to escape their teasing, Glenn ran out into the water and dived into an oncoming wave. By misjudging the depth of the water, Glenn hit the shore bottom. The impact of the dive broke his neck. His life would never be the same.

The whirlwind of a personal crisis will alter your normal pattern of life. You will never be the same after the experience. For better or worse, a crisis experience will always change you.

## The Crisis of Divorce

Divorce is a crisis experience. This fact might seem obvious to you. But many who face the crisis of divorce are so wrapped up in their emotions that they fail to recognize the nature of the experience.

We need to understand that divorce is a crisis experience. And we need to discern how the turmoil created by a divorce impacts every aspect and relationship of life.

I am reminded of Louise. She came to a Fresh Start Seminar just a few weeks after the death of her first spouse. "I know this seminar is for separated and divorced people," she noted. "But I have heard that there are similarities between death and divorce. It has been so difficult to deal with my husband's death. Perhaps I could learn something if I attended your seminar."

Louise was encouraged by her attendance at Fresh Start. However, when she returned to the seminar six months later, she came as a divorced alumnus. In the time between the two programs she had met a man, married him, then separated, and finally divorced him.

You can imagine that the second seminar took on a whole new meaning! Louise had experienced the crisis of divorce. During the seminar, she remarked, "When you lose your spouse through death, it is extremely painful. But the separation is complete, and it is socially acceptable. Like a surgeon who makes an incision with a scalpel, death's separation is neat and clean.

"It is not that way with divorce, however. Marital separation is not complete. You continue to see your former spouse through various levels of contact. And divorce is not socially acceptable. Unlike the experience of losing my first husband, I didn't receive one casserole or condolence card after the divorce. I think of divorce like the vicious slice of an attacker's knife. The wound is not clean; it is jagged and uneven.

"My experience tells me that there are many similarities between death and divorce. Divorce is the death of a relationship. But it is rarely decisive or complete. It creates an open wound. I have found it much more emotionally devastating than the death of my first husband."

In sharing the story of Louise I do not intend to debate the similarities and differences between death and divorce. Rather, I want to underline this truth that is so easily forgotten: divorce is a crisis experience. It affects every aspect of life. Therefore, divorce must be treated as a crisis.

## Handling the Divorce Crisis

A crisis is often characterized by the feeling that things seem to be out of your control. And there is some real truth to that feeling. During a divorce, the circumstances of your life are often out of your hands. Although you cannot control most of what is happening, you can strive to handle your response to the things taking place.

At the beginning of this chapter I shared the story of Peter, whose entire life seemed to collapse as a result of his divorce. However, there is more to his story. For two years Peter lived as a victim of his circumstances. Because of the rejection from others that he perceived, Peter responded in anger. He felt this anger toward the people in church who no longer talked with him. He was angry with his former wife for leaving him. The loss of his home made him angry. And he responded in anger when he was forced to abandon his career goal of entering the ministry.

After two years, Peter decided that his circumstances were not going to change. He began to accept responsibility for his future. He also changed the way he treated other people. He made a special effort to reestablish contact with his family.

Peter's mother and father had a difficult time handling his divorce. They were deeply hurt and upset by the event. After all, no one in their family had ever gone through a divorce. As a result they seemed to say all the wrong things. Peter still remembers storming out of the house when they said, "What shall we tell the relatives?"

Peter's anger toward his parents was strong. He said, "Mom and Dad never talked to me about my struggles. So I vowed never to be close to them again. They had hurt me. I would never give them another opportunity to do that. I decided to shut them, and anyone else who acted like them, out of my life."

After this extended period of anger, Peter began to see that he was the one suffering the most from his self-imposed exile. For the first time he realized how his parents had taken his divorce as their personal failure. Eventually, he was able to talk with them about their mutual reactions to his divorce. This restoration of their relationship made them closer than they had been prior to the breakup of Peter's marriage.

Peter learned what it meant to accept responsibility for his response to the divorce. However, it is clear from his experience that many people often find themselves unprepared to cope with their intense reactions to a marriage breakup. Normal methods of handling pressure are simply not adequate.

Because common coping mechanisms do not always work during the divorce experience, it is often necessary to draw on other resources and explore new methods to handle the crisis. These methods may require the development of new friendships or an entirely new support system. The members of your old support system may not understand what you are going through. They may even avoid or reject you due to loyalty to your former spouse.

Jill Stevens shares how a small group of ladies

provided a context that helped her handle the crisis of separation. "I attended a Fresh Start seminar last fall. A number of us in our small group decided to continue meeting after the seminar. These ladies have become some of my closest friends. I had tried to share with others what I was going through during the separation. I received many different reactions and all kinds of advice. But when I met with my small group, each of us shared how we were dealing with our divorce experience. Some had been divorced for quite a while. They provided a sense of hope and direction. Others were going through the same things I was facing. We could share our mistakes, or solutions that seemed to work. And when someone in the group said she was praying for me, I knew that she was really praying. She wasn't just trying to be nice."

Kevin Thompson also learned to develop new resources to cope with his divorce. He had grown up in a home where everyone had to be nice to each other. He learned at an early age that he was to keep his anger to himself. After his divorce, Kevin learned that it wasn't so easy to keep a lid on his anger. Later, in reflection, he even admitted that he used the legal process of divorce as a weapon against his former wife.

During Fresh Start, Kevin learned that he must honestly face his anger. He began to see a counselor who helped him develop constructive methods for anger management. It wasn't easy to break old habits. But Kevin's hard work paid off. During custody hearings, he was able to go out to lunch with his ex and actually listen to her concerns without negatively expressing his anger. Today his relationship with her is still unsettled, but they are able to work together constructively for the sake of their children.

## Growth Through Crisis

Perhaps you know that the Chinese symbol for crisis is two-faced: one character stands for catastrophe, and the other stands for opportunity. Our tendency is to look only at the negative side of a crisis. But each crisis also provides the opportunity for personal growth. As a matter of fact, personal maturity is, in a large measure, the result of successful crisis resolutions.

An interesting theme seems to be restated repeatedly by persons who have successfully negotiated the hazards of divorce recovery. It sounds something like this: "Going through my divorce was a terrible experience. I would never want to go through another one. Nor would I wish it on my worst enemy. But I would not trade what the experience has done for me. It has forced me to become stronger, more secure, and more mature."

This sounds similar to some of the initial thoughts shared by the apostle James in his epistle. He wrote,

When all kinds of trials and temptations crowd
into your lives, my brothers, don't resent them as
intruders, but welcome them as friends! Realize
that they come to test your faith and to produce in
you the quality of endurance. But let the process
go on until that endurance is fully developed, and
you will find you have become men of mature
character, men of integrity with no weak spots
(James 1:2–4 PHILLIPS).

Paul Roberts never would have believed his divorce meant anything but disaster in his life. He
had done everything he knew to keep the marriage
together. It was not until his former spouse remarried five years after the divorce that he felt there
was no chance for reconciliation. Nine years have
passed since the judge signed the divorce decree.
It has been difficult for Paul to adjust to the single
life. As he explains it, "I didn't have any seminars
or support groups to turn to when I was going
through my divorce. I just muddled through and
made a great many dumb mistakes. But I have
tried to learn from my mistakes. In the process, I
have also learned to accept myself. I guess I've
come to understand what forgiveness is all about.
I hated my divorce, but I'm a better man because
of it."

There it is again. The truth that difficulties and
hassles can make us better people. This is particularly true for those who believe in the personal
God who has made Himself known in the Bible.

When one knows that God is in control, crisis can become a divinely designed opportunity.

## The Human Side of Divorce

We have seen that divorce is a crisis experience. The critical issue is how one decides to handle the real and present challenges that come from crisis.

One other thing must be remembered. People—individual human beings—experience divorce. If you have been through a divorce and are reading this, you know what I mean. Perhaps you have felt as though a big *D* was sewn onto your clothes. You have felt like a statistic. And you question whether people respect you any longer. Suddenly you are labeled DIVORCED. It seems as though a hundred assumptions are drawn concerning your character.

The "people element" is often forgotten in the statistics and arguments related to divorce. Since real people face the complex challenge of marital disruption, divorce must be viewed from a perspective beyond the issues causing it. The confusion, trauma, grief, guilt, and anxiety associated with divorce must be considered. The whirlwind of divorce must be understood as an experience from which a person needs to recover and grow.

# CHAPTER TWO

# The Mating Game

"It happened again last weekend. Another couple at church became engaged. They've known each other for five months. The pastor asked them to come for premarital counseling, but they really don't think they need it. Boy, I sure hope they know what they are doing."

Carol was sharing this with some of her friends. She had walked those familiar engagement tracks before . . . five and a half years ago. Now she is single again. Her thoughts point to a profound social problem. In a society where it is easier to get married than it is to get a driver's license, one often wonders if people know what they are doing when they get married.

### Why Marriage?

Why do most people get married? The popular answer is heard in the songs and seen on the screens: "I'm in love." Love. It is considered the ultimate criterion for marriage. After all, who can argue with a couple when they say those magic words?

Divorce statistics will argue with them! And Carol, the woman mentioned above, joins with the thousands of divorced persons who quietly argue against the simplistic rationale for marriage encompassed in those four words, "We are in love."

Most people in our culture marry for romantic-passionate reasons. The result is that the more serious aspects of marital choice and marital expectation are not only neglected but sometimes ridiculed (Gansei quoted by Wright, 1971).

A friend of mine recently refused to marry a couple because they hadn't known each other more than a few weeks. They were outraged at his decision. After all, they were in love!

Our modern dream is that love will conquer all. However, reality states that love will fade and all the blemishes of real life will take over. Love—at least romantic love—is not a sufficient reason to get married.

There is a deeper reason why people marry. It is found in the first few pages of the Bible. Marriage is God ordained. God said to a listening universe, "It is not good that man should be alone" (Gen. 2:18). So He created woman as a complement to man.

Man was created in the image of God. Part of

this image-bearing nature is man's need for relationship. After all, God exists in relationship: "In the beginning was the Word, and the Word was with God, and the Word was God" (John 1:1). Man, patterned after the image of God, needs relationships as well.

This relational need is illustrated by the desperate problem of loneliness in our society. In 1972, Harvard sociologist Robert Weiss edited a book entitled *Loneliness* in which he pinpointed this problem as being of epidemic proportions in our society. In the years that have passed since this book was published, this truth has been repeatedly affirmed.

Talk to a custodial single parent if you want to understand this problem of loneliness. Helen Davies is the mother of three children, ages four to eleven. She was divorced three years ago. Although Helen would prefer to stay home with her children, she must work a full-time job to meet her family's needs. Whenever she has a few precious "free" moments, all Helen wants to do is collapse! She could spend more time with friends, but she rarely does so. Her energy level is too low to take any initiative. Yet, Helen wishes that she could talk with some adults outside the context of work.

Our need for others is not met solely through marriage. We can have fulfilling relationships with close friends, relatives, and associates. Nevertheless, the reason so many people marry and remarry stems from the desire to satisfy the natural craving for a person of ultimate significance in life.

Not long ago our family kept an inmate for a week in our home. He was participating in a community service project under the direction of Prison Fellowship. He shared with me, "You know, being out for two weeks has been difficult. I have been free, but not free to see my wife. I have felt a deep loneliness during this project because I have deeply felt the absence of Ruth." For this inmate, the opportunity to be out of prison without his "significant other" was a questionable freedom. He wanted that special person!

## The Coupling Process

When a man and a woman are drawn together into a relationship, we call the process "coupling." In our society the coupling process takes place in three broad phases: dating, engagement and marriage.

Dating can vary in commitment from a casual date to serious or steady dating. The phenomenon of dating as we know it has evolved to its current form since the end of World War I. Prior to that time, dating was highly formal, carefully chaperoned, and limited to one's town and social stratum. Since the 1920s, dating has become the socially accepted method of early coupling and mate selection.

The other day my son was asking me about my first date. "How old were you, Dad?" "What was her name?" "What did you do together?" I remembered that I was in the seventh grade, her name was Ann, and we went to a movie. No big deal, except for the fact that my first date pushed me into that strange realm of dealing with the opposite sex. I had also begun that scary process of establishing myself in the social jungle of my peer group. The older we grew, the more defined became our dating patterns and procedures. In the back of our minds we all knew this ritual was supposed to lead us to our future mate.

Dating can be a great experience. It can also be complex, terrifying, and disastrous to one's self-esteem. The pressures exerted in the dating phase often restrict true friendship development. One rarely exposes the true self on a date. Instead, roles of an ideal self are played. Therefore, dating often forms a superficial foundation for relational development.

The second phase in the coupling process is engagement, the public declaration of marriage intent. In our culture, engagement tends to be a strange mixture of wedding preparations, the contemplation of a future life together, and an absorption in the rarefied atmosphere of romance ("He really loves me!" "She wants to marry me!").

Often during engagement so much energy is poured into the wedding plans that little time and strength are left for a deepened understanding of one's future mate. Therefore, relational commitment is delayed for social expediency.

The final phase in the coupling process is marriage itself, the legal binding of the relationship. Whether stated before a minister or a justice of the peace, the marriage ceremony always includes a personal statement of faithfulness and commitment to the responsibilities involved in partnership. Of course most couples are so caught up in the excitement of the moment that they never really listen to what they are saying in these vows (let alone ponder the implications).

There are many facets to this coupling process. But in this chapter my focus shall be on what is taking place in the souls of these two people as they move through these socially accepted phases.

## Bonding

The experience of becoming bonded to another person is different from the experience of coupling. We have seen that coupling is the process of two people being drawn together into a relationship that, if continued, often concludes in marriage.

On the other hand, bonding is the slow, often unnoticed process whereby partners become mutually dependent. The Bible describes this as "becoming one flesh" (Gen. 2:24). This developing dependency occurs on every level of the human experience: emotional, social, and spiritual. In the deepest sense the couple become "attached" to each other.

One young woman who came to the office to talk to me had been married for six years. Her divorce had been finalized one year after a stormy two-and-a-half-year separation. Recently she had had dinner with her ex to talk about some financial arrangements. Ever since that dinner she had pondered whether she should try to get back together with him. She understood that her marriage was destructive. Yet she had been haunted by thoughts of reconciliation. She shared with me that she felt a little crazy. What could she do about it? As we talked, I told her that bonding goes much deeper than ink on a piece of paper. Marriage partners' lives become intertwined, and the unraveling of these bonds is not easy.

A friend of mine is employed by a major telecommunications company. He works in a plant that produces heavy long-line cables. These cables are made up of hundreds of small lines that are twisted together, and it is very difficult for them to be taken apart. A bonded relationship is much like one of these cables. Slowly, two people become emotionally entwined. As they share their lives over time, the bonding process takes place. Their souls come together.

Another way to describe bonding is the feeling
you are "at home" when you are with that special
person. An example of this is found in that wonderful musical *Fiddler on the Roof*. One theme of
the play is the romance between Tevia's daughter
Huddle and her gentile lover, Pocheck. Pocheck is
sent to Siberia as punishment for causing political
unrest. Huddle decides that she must leave her
family and move to Siberia to be with her beloved
Pocheck. As she prepares to leave her family, she
sings "Far From the Home I Love." This song describes the difficulty she has leaving her family
and community. However, the last line of the song
summarizes her bondedness with Pocheck. Huddle concludes, "There with my love, I'm home."

"Home is where the heart is." It is an old line,
but the message remains true. Bonding is the coming together of hearts in interpersonal union. People feel at home with those to whom they are
bonded.

The bonds formed between two partners can become very strong. John Bowlby, who has studied
the bonding process extensively, states, "Many of
the most intense emotions occur during the development, growth, disruption, and renewal of the
bonding process" (Bowlby, 1973).

The intensity of marital bonding between husband and wife is illustrated in a situation in which
I was involved. A man was continually abusing his
spouse, emotionally and physically. Week after
week stretched into year after year of abuse suf-

fered by this woman. There were times when she sought help. But in a short period of time she would always withdraw her request. The friends who heard her pleas would always assume that things worked out and the marriage was fine.

When we hear the story of this abused wife, we ask, "Why was this poor woman willing to endure such a terrible situation? Why did she remain with her husband by withdrawing her requests for help?" One part of the answer to these questions is found in the intense attachment of the bonding between them.

# CHAPTER THREE

# Till Death Do Us Part

## (The Decision to Divorce)

For Bob, there was no choice—simply a response. His wife had left him. He had to decide what he would do about it. In the end he signed the divorce decree, even though he didn't agree with it.

For Marcia, it was a matter of facing the truth of her husband's unfaithfulness. She concluded, "You can play the game only so long. Then you must come to grips with what is really taking place. I had confronted him so many times with the facts. Finally, I divorced him. I felt it was an honest response to his lying."

In Diane's case the divorce decision came out of the cycle of separation, reconciliation, and reseparation. Like two bloodied fighters, Diane and her husband decided to call a truce. They mutually agreed that divorce was the answer.

A popular song on the radio plays that woeful refrain, "Doesn't anybody ever stick together anymore?" You wonder if anyone ever does!

Why is divorce so prevalent? What brings a person, or a couple, to the point of calling it quits with marriage?

Psychologists and sociologists have conducted all types of studies in an attempt to explain divorce. Yet, after their data have been quantified and examined, their conclusions won't help a couple on the verge of breaking up.

Preachers say that divorce is a result of the lack of responsibility and commitment in our culture. And there is a good bit of truth in that statement. God considers marriage a lifelong commitment. And a quick survey of history proves that a society's condoning of divorce strikes at the moral fiber of the community.

Still, after all the talk about responsibility, commitment, and moral fiber, the pain driving a husband and wife to the verge of separation is rarely understood.

"Well," some say, "the answer must be sin. Divorce is the result of sin." Yes, that is correct. Every problem in society can be traced back to this root issue. However, it is one thing to recognize the reality of sin and quite another to do something about its consequences.

Pat answers about the problem of divorce are easy to find. They provide simplistic solutions. They also shield those who use them from the lives and circumstances of real people. The person who uses pat answers will find a way to fit every divorce into his own formula. However, this is not fair. Each divorce has a unique chemistry all its own. Therefore, each divorce defies pat answers and easy solutions.

## Common Reasons for Divorce

There are no easy answers to explain what leads a couple to separate. The path to divorce is a long one, winding through complex issues and complicated events. To discover the real reasons for each divorce, one must spend time reviewing a couple's dating background and marital history.

However, it is possible to review some common links in the chain of events that adversely affect the solidarity of a marriage. If these links are examined, one may be able to learn something of his own experiences.

The following are five common reasons why many seek a divorce. Perhaps some of them will sound familiar to you in your own circumstances.

### 1. No Longer Friends

"At one time I thought that Nancy was my best friend. But over the years we have drifted apart. Now I consider others as much closer friends than my own wife."

This is the reason Gene gave for his divorce. He was putting in long hours on a project with his coworker Marie. To wind down, they would go out to lunch; sometimes they shared a few drinks after work. The more time Gene spent with Marie, the more he felt they had in common. They talked the same language and shared the same dreams.

However, when Gene came home from work, he felt that his wife was disinterested in the things that concerned him. She wanted to talk only about her own problems. So, when she would start to talk, Gene would emotionally withdraw from the conversation. In the meantime, he thought a lot about Marie.

## 2. Decreased Trust

"There was a time when I trusted Jerry explicitly. But now I've experienced too much. He has shattered my trust one more time than I am willing to forget."

Margaret was sharing how Jerry, her husband of nine years, had been unfaithful to her three times in the past two years. After each affair, Jerry returned to Margaret full of remorse, vowing a recommitment to Christ and to their marriage. However, when Margaret would suggest that they go for counseling to examine the root issues of his unfaithfulness, Jerry accused her of not believing in him. He said she was questioning his sincerity. So, after Jerry's fourth affair, Margaret decided that she had taken enough of his lies. She took the initiative to go to a lawyer and begin divorce proceedings.

### 3. Poor Communication

"Mark and I used to talk about everything. . . .
Now we hardly talk at all."

Edith shared how she and Mark used to sit for
hours at their special little bookstore talking in the
coffee shop in the back. Now, after three years of
marriage, Mark rarely talked at all. He would
come home from work, eat dinner, watch television, and go to bed. Whenever Edith ventured to
strike up a conversation, Mark would say that he
was too tired or that he had talked all day. Or he
would say that he just wanted some peace and
quiet.

As Edith pressed Mark to talk, he would pull
away even more. Finally, Edith found herself
screaming at Mark. (She hadn't screamed since
she was a teenager!) Mark's response was to go
into another room.

After months and months with no change, Edith
filed for a divorce. Mark didn't contest her actions.

Another example of poor communication is seen
in Jim's experience. In a small group, Jim began to
share with great difficulty how his wife ridiculed
him in front of his friends and business associates.
However, when they were alone, Jim's wife refused
to talk with him about her criticism. As a matter of
fact, she refused to talk with him at all! Any time
Jim initiated conversation, she would turn and

walk away. It was not long before he couldn't stand this kind of treatment anymore. When Jim filed for a divorce, his wife said it was the first thing he had done in years that she was able to respect.

### 4. Lack of Shared Goals

"Once we were moving together in the same direction. Now we seem to be walking down two separate paths with different goals, different friends, and different dreams."

Dennis had become totally absorbed in his vocational pursuits. He held down two full-time jobs. And he didn't do it because he and Lorraine needed the money. He was simply absorbed in the thrill of achievement at work. He was committing nonsexual adultery, and his mistress was risk ventures and success.

Lorraine became tired of Dennis's absentee lifestyle. So she slowly established her own little world. First, it was lunch with her girlfriends at the club. Then it grew into a "relationship" with the bottle. Finally, she became addicted to both prescription and illegal drugs.

Dennis began to notice a difference in his wife. But he didn't take the time to find out what was bothering her. *After all,* he thought, *what else could she want from me? I've given her everything she could want.*

The story of Ken and Cindy is not as dramatic as that of Dennis and Lorraine, but it is just as devastating. Ken had always loved sports. Cindy found his love for athletics to be one of his most attractive characteristics. He seemed to be involved in every league in the city. Most of their dates prior to marriage centered on one of Ken's many activities: softball practice, basketball games, or football coaching for the local YMCA.

After their marriage, Cindy continued to go to all of the events with Ken. Then came the birth of their child. A second baby came quickly after the first. Suddenly, Cindy found her life absorbed in the "log cabin" syndrome of staying home with the children. Ken continued in his sports. When Cindy suggested that he rearrange his schedule so they could have some time together, Ken became angry and defensive. His extracurricular activities were nonnegotiable.

## 5. Discontinued Marital Intimacy

"He no longer seemed interested in me as a person . . . or as a lover. He would go for months at a time without even touching me. So, after a while, I just hardened myself to him."

If you had told Carol that she was going to have an affair, she would have laughed you out of the room. After all, she was a committed Christian! And she was a Bible study leader! She knew better than to do something like that.

At the same time, Carol felt a deep sense of loneliness. Her husband, Roger, seemed so critical of her. Of course he was under a great deal of stress now that the company was laying off management personnel. But their problems seemed deeper than that. He disregarded the things that really mattered to her.

On the other hand, Bruce seemed genuinely concerned for her. And to think that their relationship began over the discussion of a passage from the Bible.

Carol confessed, "I felt guilt at first. But he made me feel so good. I felt respected, needed, loved, even cute for the first time in a long time. Soon I decided it was okay to spend time with Bruce because it was meeting my needs. I reasoned, 'He's only a friend.' Before I knew what happened, I was in an affair."

## The Need for Honesty and Repentance

We have looked at five common reasons why many people seek divorce. They represent a sample of the many rationales given for marital separation.

None of the reasons noted here (nor any other reason for that matter) need precipitate a divorce. However, there is a catch if divorce is to be prevented; both spouses must admit their own problems and the differences existing in the marriage. That may or may not be hard, depending on the level of honesty each partner is able to maintain.

Willingness to acknowledge and work on problems is the first step to resolving the divorce dilemma.

Of course the hard work only begins with honesty. It must go beyond this to the point that each spouse is willing to negotiate differences and learn how to accept the unchangeable in the other.

This can be a tough job! It seems that a couple of generations ago our grandparents were trained how to "give in," overlooking personal rights for the sake of the common good. Today we learn how to stand up for our rights and get our own way. It is possible to learn how to modify this habit through honest resolution of differences for the sake of our marriage partnership. But doing that takes a real investment of time and energy.

One other thing is necessary to resolve marital differences. The Bible calls it "repentance." True repentance is not some kind of loud wailing and crying while telling it all. Rather, repentance starts with each person recognizing how he or she has made real mistakes. After this recognition, each must openly acknowledge personal mistakes to the other. Then, as partners, they must commit themselves to work together for change that will strengthen their marriage and their respect for each another.

Tom and Janet's marriage had degenerated into name calling and physical violence. Janet had finally moved out of the house to protect herself. Neither partner wanted a divorce, but they didn't seem to know how to handle their feelings. After talking over these things at lunch every day for an entire week at a restaurant (thereby controlling their feelings by not making a scene in public), both Tom and Janet committed themselves to go for counseling. They were totally candid as they discussed their problem with the counselor. After two weeks, Janet felt as though she could move home. Today they are still working hard on their marriage. And they still have fights. But the physical abuse has ended. And their fights have become quieter as they learn how to listen and respond to each another. They haven't "arrived" at a perfect marriage, but they feel good about their progress and their commitment to each another.

## The Decision to Divorce

As Jill shared in her small group at a Fresh Start Seminar, it was obvious that she was still in a state of shock. "Just three weeks ago Howard dropped the bomb on me. I had no idea that it was coming," she explained.

Even though Howard's actions surprised Jill, she soon learned that his decision was not impulsive. He had been considering it for months. As she stopped to recall the past few years, Jill began to see how the demise of her marriage came about. From the wisdom of hindsight it all fit into place.

Jill's experience conforms to a rather predictable pattern. Sometime during the marriage, one or both partners begin to conclude that their partnership is not worth the effort to keep it together.

What seems like "just a few problems" to one spouse might be the foundation for separation to the other.

### The Unconscious Decision

Keith sat across from me, relating his experience. "I really don't understand how I got to this point," he said. "I have had plenty of opportunities to be unfaithful to my wife through the years. But I always knew it was the wrong thing to do. So I hung in there . . . until I met Diane. She is everything I ever dreamed of in a friend, a companion, and a lover. In comparison to Diane, the relationship I have with my wife is just bland."

As we talked further, Keith explained how he had drifted from his wife over the years. Longer hours and more responsibility at work seemed to keep them apart. He no longer thought of his wife or did special things for her. A few months before he met Diane, he had even taken the picture of his wife out of his billfold.

Keith's actions are some typical signs of uncoupling. Over time he had moved apart from his wife. In many ways he had been preparing himself emotionally for the breakup long before the "right" opportunity for action presented itself. When Diane came into his life, Keith was ready to follow

through on the decision to leave his wife, which he
had emotionally concluded much earlier.

### The Conscious Decision

"I knew it was only a matter of time," Nancy
confided. "He was married more to his job and his
friends than he was to me. Now, don't take me
wrong. I knew that his job was important. And I
thought it was good for him to have friends. But
when I pushed him to share with me what was going on in his life, he would always retreat back to
his newspaper or to the television. After a while I
figured, 'Well, if this is all he wants out of a marriage, he can forget it.' So I started making plans
for the split. That was—what—six, maybe eight
months before I finally left him."

Nancy didn't waste any time. She made her decision and followed through with it. On the other
hand, Keith's movement toward separation was
not a deliberate decision. As far as he was concerned, Diane came into his life from "out of the
blue."

Here is the point: both Keith and Nancy made a
decision to divorce. Once this decision was
reached, the emotional investment that they had in
their respective marriages started to be withdrawn. Both of them became like exhausted swim-
mers who, gasping for air, finally lose the hope of
survival. At that point, as far as Nancy and Keith

were concerned, their marriages were stone cold dead.

## Active Agent, Passive Agent

Very few marital breakups occur with both spouses desiring a divorce at the same time. A pattern normally develops in which one spouse takes the role of the "active agent" while the other assumes the role of the "passive agent."

Jean's husband was an alcoholic. Throughout the twenty-one years of their marriage, her husband called all of the shots. Jean did anything he wanted her to do at any time. The turning point for Jean came when her husband called her while she was visiting her daughter. He wanted her to drop everything and come home. There was no emergency and no major problems. He just wanted her to come home. She replied, "No, I'll come home when I told you I would come home!" The ability to say no gave her the courage to move forward and divorce him.

If you met Jean, you would assume she was the "passive agent" in her divorce. After all, she had put up with an abusive, domineering husband for twenty-one years. Yet something rose up within her to take the divorce action against him. It is wrong to assume that the "active agent" is always the aggressive, assertive member of the couple.

The "active agent" generally leaves the marriage and files for the divorce. However, you
should not be fooled into thinking that these roles
are permanent. Spouses can switch roles! In one
case I'm familiar with, the wife left her husband.
He pleaded with her to reconcile. Finally, she
agreed to go to counseling with him. After two sessions, the husband turned around and filed for divorce against his wife.

Another illustration of a surprising active agent
can be seen in the marriage of Bill and Louise. Bill
had been using the threat of divorce to manipulate
Louise for years. Through all of the emotional
abuse, Louise stuck with her man. However, after
their last bout, culminating with Bill's typical
threat to leave, Louise decided to call his bluff. She
filed for divorce against him!

The most difficult time for the active agent is often prior to separating and filing for the divorce.
After taking these actions, the active agent views
the marriage as a past event. The individual begins
to live without the perceived "burden" of the
spouse. This is not to say that the active agent
doesn't struggle with the guilt and the implications of initiating the divorce. However, the individual accepts that the marriage is history and
recognizes the importance of getting on with life.

Dot struggled in her marriage for years. She felt
unloved and disregarded. She also felt trapped, unable to do anything about her situation. Out of her
depression she gained a resolve to go against her

family, her church, and her husband. She concluded that it would be better to be alone than to continue in such a miserable situation. Finally, she mustered the courage to tell her husband that she was leaving. He laughed at her and said, "You'll be back."

After she had left him, Dot knew she had been through the worst of it all. The divorce wasn't final, but she felt she was well on the way to independence and acceptance of her new lifestyle. Meanwhile, her husband continued to tell everyone how she would come back to him on her hands and knees.

The active agent acts out the decision to divorce. However, the passive agent lives in the fear that the foundations of life are crumbling. The passive agent often frantically tries to hold things together and will do or say almost anything to prevent the divorce. Or the passive agent will blindly assume that everything will work out and the marriage will just come back together again.

When his wife said she wasn't happy and showed less interest in him, Leroy thought it was just a phase that would go away. He prayed that Doris would feel better, but things only got worse. Despite his attempts to spend time with her, Doris seemed to grow more and more distant. Finally, she told Leroy that she didn't love him anymore. Then she left him. Leroy was shocked. Later he said, "I guess I should have seen it coming."

Another characteristic of the passive agent is

the refusal to accept the death of the marriage. The active agent may demonstrate time and again that the marriage is over, but the passive agent resists all the signals. It might take quite some time after the marriage has broken up before the passive agent is willing to accept reality.

When the active agent decides in favor of divorce and acts on this decision, the individual becomes very resistant to review or revise this decision. Regardless of shared history, family, friends, or even what the church might say, the active agent believes that the marriage is finished. Then, over a period of time, the passive agent will usually come to this conclusion as well.

The marriage might be over in the minds and hearts of a couple, but the implications of the divorce just begin to take effect. Couples in the midst of breaking up rarely understand what divorce does to the people who are involved. Often they simply consider it as their "ticket to ride" for freedom and a new life. However, in the last chapter we learned that marriage creates a one-flesh relationship. When a divorce takes place between two bonded people, it sends them into a whirlwind that will have an immediate and long-term impact on their lives. In the next chapter we will explore what divorce does to two people who have been in a bonded relationship.

# CHAPTER FOUR

# The Ripping Apart of One Flesh

"I know that it was my decision to divorce Don. But I never thought that it would be this hard."

"Don't let anybody ever kid you. I thought getting a divorce would solve my problems. Well, divorce might ease the pain temporarily, but it isn't a simple answer to resolve life's hassles. I have to work harder at dealing with my ex than I ever did when we were together."

"My husband said that he was stupid. He dumped me for another woman. Now he tells me that she is ten times worse to him that I ever was. I wanted to have him back—but now he has remarried. He has got what he deserved! Still, that doesn't make it any easier for me and the kids."

These are the thoughts of a few people who have gone through the breakup of a bonded relationship. You remember that in chapter 2 we talked about bonding: that process ordained by God in Genesis 2 whereby two people become attached. In this passage God said that a husband and a wife should leave father and mother, cleave to each other, and become one flesh.

Once a friend of mine had two of his fingers bonded together with one of those tremendously strong glues. This was prior to the sale of a solvent for the stuff! You talk about pain. Getting his fingers unstuck was a slow and agonizing process. Consider the fact that God describes marriage partners as "one flesh." God uses the word *cleave* in Genesis 2 to describe this one-flesh condition. The word for *cleave* in Hebrew actually means "to be glued together"! Therefore, divorce means that two glued partners in the one-flesh relationship are being torn apart.

## A Slow and Painful Process

The breaking of the one-flesh relationship bond can be a very slow and painful process. The attachment one has to a spouse can remain long after the decision to divorce. Paul, a domestic attorney, relates a story he has found rather common in his practice. A middle-aged woman comes into his office. Her husband left her and has taken the initial steps for a divorce. Will Paul represent her in the suit?

Paul responds with his normal request: "Please share a brief history of your marriage and how you have come to the point of divorce." The woman proceeds with a long and involved story emphasizing the problems and failures of her husband. He is a villain; she is the innocent victim. By the end of her presentation one could believe that she was married to a reincarnation of Adolf Hitler.

My attorney friend Paul then restates the highlights of her story to clarify his understanding of what she has shared. As Paul summarizes her statements, the prospective client begins to defend her estranged spouse! He has to remind her that he is only restating what she has said. "Oh," she exclaims, "did I really say that? I didn't know I was being so hard on him."

What was taking place in my friend's law office? The woman was betraying her ambivalence. On the one hand, she was feeling real pain and honest hurt. The man whom she had trusted had betrayed her! On the other hand, she still felt a deep attachment to him. So she defended his character.

Isn't this the way it is with family? Two siblings can scream their lungs out at each other. But if you really want a fight, let an outsider criticize one brother to the other!

Marital bondedness fades slowly. And to make matters worse, the pain created by the brokenness of the marriage bond is compounded by the impact of divorce on almost every other area of life. You see, divorce acts something like a personal volcano, disrupting virtually every aspect of personal and interpersonal experience.

Psychologist Gloria Gray (1978) conducted a

study on the impact of divorce on people's lives. Her findings are quite revealing. She reports that divorce produces loneliness, disorganization, low work efficiency, unhappiness, increased use of alcohol and tobacco, and extreme weight change. Her conclusion is both simple and profound: "the person who did not experience change in one or more of these areas during separation was rare."

Victor would agree with Gloria Gray. He says, "If it were not for a boss who understood what I was going through, I would have been canned. For a period of about six months, I was basically worthless to the company. I would come to the office and push papers on my desk. I was so disoriented and involved in my personal problems that I couldn't concentrate at all."

Continued bondedness to the former partner and the disruption of almost every area of life— these are the realities of divorce. But they do not stand alone. In addition to these problems, one must face critical life decisions during this period of disorientation. For example, many women face the prospect of having to find a job after separation. Jan was one of these women. She had a college degree, but she hadn't worked for fifteen years. And child rearing wasn't listed in the want ads! It took some time—and some long talks with close friends—before she started the job hunting process.

There is also the need to find a new place to live. Very often the terms of a divorce require that the mutually owned home be sold and the assets split between the parties. Suddenly you (and perhaps your children) are uprooted from familiar surroundings and forced to deal with a new neighborhood, a new school, and a different environment.

Together with these changes come the financial adjustments. And you are required to inform the whole world (including your relatives and friends) that you are now single. And there is that "little" matter of retaining a lawyer and facing litigation. (Do you realize that most people facing a divorce have never even seen the inside of a courtroom, let alone hired an attorney?)

Perhaps, for parents, the most difficult adjustment is with the children. For the custodial parent, the difficulties are in coping with parenting as a single. You are required to carry the primary responsibility of helping your children handle the divorce. For the noncustodial parent, there is the struggle of learning how to live without your children. Perhaps you never realized how important the children were to you until the marriage broke up.

## Why Does It All Hurt So Bad?

So much for the litany of problems facing persons who divorce. If you have been or are going through marital separation, you understand the difficulties better than any researcher! However, the problem remains. Why is divorce so painful? And why does it take so much time to get over it?

In chapter 1, separation and divorce was defined as the whirlwind of a crisis experience. We also observed that divorce was very similar to experiencing the death of a loved one. And divorce is a death—the death of a relationship! Yet it is different from the physical death of a spouse.

Consider Emily's experience. She lost her first husband to cancer. Of course, it was hard to lose Bob. But she did have her family, her friends, and her church. She recounts, "I had people sending me cards; people bringing casseroles to my home; people calling me and asking how I was doing."

Two years after Bob's death, Emily married Allen. He divorced her after eighteen months of marriage. This time there were no cards, no casseroles, and no telephone calls. Emily remembers, "When I was divorced, I felt like I was Public Enemy #1. Of course, one reason for those feelings was the way I viewed myself. Still, I didn't seem to receive any support until Randy and Barbara let me move into their home for a few months. With their help, and the encouragement of a Bible study group we were in, I seemed to muddle through."

Emily experienced real grief as a result of her divorce. Her grief was similar to what she had experienced when her first husband, Bob, died a few years earlier. But the grief after her divorce was more like an open wound. Allen, her second husband, continued to live in the same city after their separation. Their divorce trial was full of anger and differences that deepened and prolonged the pain. Even after the divorce they bickered and clashed with each other. They didn't want to be together, but for some strange reason they kept in contact and conflict. Their bondedness didn't die easily.

However, there is another reason why the breaking of the one-flesh relationship between Emily and Allen created deep pain. It has to do with God's investment in their marriage. We saw in chapter 2 that marriage is God ordained. Further, God considers marriage a covenant. The word *covenant* seems rather strange and archaic to us. It is not used often outside the religious realm. Yet the idea behind a covenant is not unusual to our society at all.

Most of us have signed some type of contract. We do this when we buy a car or rent an apartment or purchase an airline ticket. A contract is simply an agreement between two parties: one usually agrees to make a payment; the other delivers some goods or services for the payment.

Think of a covenant as a relationship contract. It is an agreement between two people to develop and maintain a special kind of relationship.

Consider the covenant made by two little boys playing cowboys and Indians in the backyard. During their play, they agree to be "blood brothers."

They might even pretend to symbolizing a min-
gling of blood, they mutually commit themselves
to each other. They have made a covenant.

In the Bible we read of David and Jonathan.
These two young men were best friends. They
sealed their friendship by making promises to
each other and by sharing a mutual responsibility
to sustain their friendship. Finally, they acknowledged the punishment that should take place if either of them violated the commitment. They made
a covenant. (See 1 Sam. 20:12–23, 41–42.)

If you sign a contract and fail to meet the obliga-
tions stated in that contract, you are liable to the
penalties applicable to your violation. One day I
responded to a knock at my door. It was a man
from a collection agency coming to confiscate a
car! Apparently someone had given the auto deal-
ership my address, and the dealer had failed to
pick out the deception in the credit check. When
this person failed to make payments on his car,
they were quickly taking action to enforce their
rights under the contract. (But I didn't let them
take my car!)

In a similar way, when two people break a relationship covenant, they will always experience
painful consequences due to the violation of their
commitment. The apostle Peter even applies these
consequences to one's prayer life. He states, "Husbands, . . . dwell with [your wives] with understanding, . . . that your prayers may not be

hindered" (1 Pet. 3:7). Apparently, improper treatment of a spouse will affect the spiritual life of the violator.

Therefore, we shouldn't be surprised by the pain accompanying the one-flesh break of divorce, even when the marriage has produced much difficulty and heartbreak. God has factored in pain as a natural condition of covenant breaking.

## Dealing with the Pain

Our tendency is to avoid pain as much as possible. Most of us would consider people who enjoy pain to be emotionally ill. However, if we stop and think about it, pain can be an invaluable asset to those who understand it.

Dr. Paul Bryant is a world-famous physician who specializes in the treatment of leprosy. In his work he has learned the value of pain. Because leprosy destroys the nerves in the infected area of a patient's body, the individual cannot feel pain where the infection has spread. Furthermore, if the patient injures an infected area (like his hands or his feet), the injury may go unnoticed since he feels no pain. Often, the complications arising from such an injury become more serious than the leprosy itself. We can see why Dr. Bryant has learned to be thankful for pain, which plays a key preventive and corrective role in the human body.

In a similar way, the Bible teaches that emotional pain, while never good in and of itself (Heb. 12:11), can be of benefit in the results that it produces. The Swiss physician Paul Tournier explained this in his book *Creative Suffering*. Here he wrote, "Deprivation and suffering is not the cause of growth, but rather its occasion. The distinction is a subtle one, of course, but it is vital."

Consider the role of pain in the divorce experience. There is no doubt that a marriage and family breakup hurts everyone involved. How shall this hurt be handled? Running from the pain will only prolong its impact. However, honestly dealing with the real hurt of marital disruption can be beneficial. If you are willing to accept the challenge of facing your pain honestly, the remaining portions of this book will help you work at making your divorce experience an occasion for growth rather than one of emotional crippling.

## The Necessity of Mourning

The dictionary defines *mourning* as the "ability to feel or express grief or sorrow." When we hear the word *mourning*, we generally think of it in terms of death. For example, we hear on television the desperate cry of a mother when she learns her child was mortally struck by a car. Or we remember the quiet sobbing of an adult son when his mother finally succumbs to a fatal illness.

We have learned that divorce is a different kind of death. It is the death of a relationship. However, as with any death, divorce creates the need to mourn. Divorce produces real grief that must be owned and experienced.

You might understand your need to mourn. You might know that you should face the impact of your loss or rejection. However, this understanding will not deter or speed up the mourning process. Paula, a therapist, learned this from firsthand experience. She shared, "I am a mental health professional. I have been dealing with the realities of grief all of my professional life. However, in going through my divorce, I have had to experience grief personally. I had studied it and shared the pain of others going through it. But it is an entirely different experience to go through the grief yourself."

Of course, no one likes to grieve. Each one of us would like to avoid it, or at least resolve it as quickly as possible. But, there is no such thing as quick grief. The process must go on until the emotional convalescence is complete.

## The Patterns of Grief

Grief is always part of a crisis experience. Any kind of crisis—whether it means facing surgery, failing to receive an anticipated promotion, or dealing with death or divorce—brings grief. Therefore, when we face grief, it is helpful to understand that we tend to cope with it in a rather predictable pattern.

The patterns of grief are often presented using a model of grieving stages. One of the best-known models is found in the book *On Death and Dying* by Dr. Elisabeth Kübler-Ross.

When it comes to the topic of divorce, no less than twelve different models of emotional grieving stages have been suggested by as many authors. But when we look at the basic components of these models, the essential differences between them are minor. The five-stage model that Dr. Kübler-Ross has popularized expresses the grief of divorce very well. Therefore, in the following chapters, we will use this model to understand how the emotions coming from the divorce experience can be handled in a responsible and God-honoring fashion.

However, as we begin our study, we must consider an important point: a model of grieving stages will package mourning into nice, neat compartments. Yet in real life, the experience of grief is not so neat and easy. You often feel like you are riding on an emotional roller coaster!

Therefore, we will be looking at these stages as they are outlined on the *slippery slope*. The idea of the slippery slope came from an experience I had as a cadet at Virginia Military Institute. Two groups of us were marched to a deep pit that had been thoroughly soaked with water. It had turned into a slimy, slippery mudhole. Four men were picked from each group and told to jump into the pit. The goal was simple: the men from one group were to get out of the pit as fast as possible while keeping the men from the other group in the pit.

You can imagine the result of this experience! As soon as one man seemed to make it to the top, a hand would reach out and grab his ankle. Suddenly he would be dragged, feet first, down to the bottom of the hole! Again and again, men who thought they would make it to the top found themselves mired in the muck of the pit.

People going through the stages of grief are like those of us in that mudhole. In the following chapters these stages are presented in an orderly manner, but actually experiencing them is like being in a mudhole. You might feel that you are finally coming to the conclusion of your emotional struggle. Then the telephone rings, and you hear from your ex. Or your child is hurt at school, and you must leave work to take care of her. Or you face an empty apartment on Saturday night. Bam! You are back in the pit again.

So, as you read, keep in mind that the experience of grief is more "muddy" than the description of it. Stages can mix and mingle together into an emotional blur. Where you are on the slippery slope generally depends on what stage you seem to dwell on the most.

Well, now it is time to begin. Jump into the pit with me as we begin to explore the slippery slope. We will start with a look at denial.

# CHAPTER FIVE

# Putting Off Until Tomorrow What I Don't Want Today
## *(The Experience of Denial)*

November 22, 1963. Ask a person who was at least five years old on that date and he can probably tell you what he was doing the moment he heard that President John F. Kennedy had been shot.

At the first mention of President Kennedy's assassination the common responses were shock, surprise, and disbelief. "That's not possible in this country," some said. "Who would believe that could happen in this day and age?" others commented.

Each of these responses is an expression of denial. Denial, very simply, occurs when we don't want to face a fact or circumstance that we know is true. So we do what we can to avoid the reality and act as if it is not there.

Denial is part of our God-given emotional pain network. It serves as a "shock absorber" while a person attempts to maintain normalcy in the midst of abnormal pressures. It often provides a momentary escape from difficult circumstances by nourishing the secret hope that "all of this is a bad dream."

## The Denial of Divorce

It was at the very end of a Fresh Start Seminar when a woman approached me. She had a troubled look on her face. "I'm so sorry," she explained. "When the church first started to have this seminar a few years ago, I was one of the chief critics. I thought that we were condoning divorce. *After all,* I thought, *if a person is growing in Christ, divorce should never happen!* Then my husband left. . . ." She broke into tears and paused for a moment before she went on. "I never understood . . . I can't believe that this is happening to me."

That is the recurrent phrase of denial: "I can't believe that this is happening to me." Each person who says it knows that the marital separation is truly taking place. But it seems so disjointed from the individual's expectations for life and marriage. Life seems to be like a surrealist painting. Everything within the person's system says, "No! This should not be taking place."

Denial is a reaction to circumstances that are beyond one's control. It is an attempt to isolate oneself against reality and all of the pain that is taking place.

I am reminded of the time I visited a family in the hospital. Their son was dying from an overdose of drugs. The mother was crying uncontrollably in the hospital lobby. The boy's grandfather was holding the mother and saying to her, "Stop crying! Stop crying! We've got to be strong. Stop crying!"

I am sure that the boy's grandfather meant well in his intent. But his exhortation betrayed the method he was using to cope with his emotions. He was pushing the feelings down, trying not to experience the pain, trying to be "strong."

In Mark 8:32 we find an example of denial in the life of Peter. Jesus had just spoken of His coming death. He explained that He must suffer many things and be rejected by the elders, chief priests, and teachers of the law. He had said that He must be killed and after three days rise again. This was too much for Peter. None of it fit into his preconceived understanding of Jesus' purpose. Therefore, he refused to believe the Lord. He even rebuked Christ for speaking in that way. In his denial he would not listen to the truth.

I once approached a friend who was going through a divorce and greeted him with a friendly, "How are you doing?" Now, we all know that this is a nice way of saying, "Hello." Rarely do people really want to know how you are doing. However, I am grateful that my friend took me seriously.

He said, "Well, I go to work and try to close out everything else that is happening to me. I seem to handle myself pretty well while I am there. But when I get out to the car to go home, it all hits me again: my wife is gone; my kids are gone. And I know that when I put my key into the lock in our door tonight, no one will be there to greet me."

My friend continued to share: "A few days ago I was cleaning the house. Everything seemed to be fine until I came across one of my son's blocks. I haven't seen him since his mother left. . . . I just broke down."

The fact that he was separated was all too obvious to my friend. Yet he tried to stay in denial because it was safe and comfortable. However, the truth would not allow him to remain there.

## The Shock of a Crisis

In her book *Mourning Song,* Joyce Landorf explains that denial is like a special oxygen mask to use when the whirlwind of a crisis has sucked every ounce of air out of us. We breathe in the breath of denial, and it seems to help us maintain some normalcy in life.

It is okay to use denial as a temporary means of escape. There are times when individuals can't deal with the intense pain of the moment. However, if denial is used as an ongoing method of coping with divorce, it can produce destructive results. People who dwell in denial can become superficial and dishonest. They often look for the easy way out instead of coming to terms with the truth.

Prolonged use of denial can actually hinder a person from the ability to handle real life. Therefore, the use of denial must be temporary, like the use of a handrail when you slip on the stairs. Denial is a quick way of regaining emotional equilibrium.

Once, while speaking on denial, I mentioned an experience shared by Jim Smoke in his book *Growing Through Divorce*. Jim said that he was talking to a group about denial. Suddenly a wedding ring flew past his nose, hit the wall behind him, and rolled back to a point near the podium. He bent down and picked up the wedding ring. Then he asked, "Does this belong to someone in here?" From the back of the room came a reply: "It did belong to me. But I have been divorced now for over six years. I guess it's about time that I took it off."

After I shared this story at a seminar, a small group leader came up to me with a smile on his face. He said, "I could relate to that story. For over a year after my divorce I kept my wedding ring on my finger, except when I was on a date. I wanted people—especially people at work—to think that I was still married."

This is denial. Putting up a facade for your friends, your acquaintances, and yourself. It is creating a fantasy world where things are so much better than what they really are in your life.

A person need not go on a guilt trip for using denial. It is a natural and normal method of initially handling shock. After an auto accident, one's body often goes into shock. During a crisis, one's emotional system does the same thing. It is helpful to know that it is okay to be in denial.

However, denial must be considered an initial, short-term method of coping. One of the difficult things that must be faced in the early phase of a crisis is that problems are never solved by shutting one's eyes. As the Living Bible paraphrases Jeremiah 6:14, "You can't heal a wound by saying it's not there!"


## Facing Denial

When I was in college, I heard a man whom I respected a great deal make the following statement: "We must turn from the unchangeable past in order to confront the inexorable future." When I first heard him say this, I was impressed by his use of language. But I didn't understand what he had said! In particular, I didn't know what *inexorable* meant. So I turned to the dictionary. There I read that *inexorable* means "not to be changed or persuaded; relentless."

Then I was able to grasp the meaning of this man's statement. First, he was stating that it is difficult for us to turn away from our unchangeable past. We often hear of people who are still living in the past by either basking in former glory or blaming their present condition on past problems. We must turn from this mind-set if we are going to live responsibly.

Second, this man was stating that we must face the inexorable (relentless) future. This can be just as difficult as leaving the past! We want to hide from the future rather than face it head-on.

Learning to apply this statement is critical for the person who is working through denial. By turning from the unchangeable past, I do not mean we must push aside the lessons we have learned from previous experiences. Rather, we must accept what has taken place in the past, learn from it, and move on with our lives.

I think of Louise, a young woman who grew up in an extremely abusive home. Now in her late twenties, Louise is coming to grips with the detrimental impact that her past experiences have had on her present life. However, she also has learned to accept responsibility for her daily thoughts and actions. In accepting this responsibility, she has learned to integrate her past difficulties into present growth rather than use the past as an alibi for a refusal to change and mature. By turning from the unchangeable past, Louise is learning how to face the temptation of continuing to live in denial.

We also need to confront the inexorable future. After all, our fear of the future and the relative security we find in the status quo of the past cause us to use denial. Change is never comfortable. And the greater the change, the higher is the level of our discomfort. However, change can also bring growth. So it is actually the unknown that threatens us. To handle denial, we must accept our fear and our lack of comfort. It takes a calculated risk. Putting off the decision to change may mean temporary comfort. Sooner or later the facts must be faced. And most divorced persons usually admit that they should have faced the unpleasant realities sooner rather than later.

Ralph spent four years fighting against the divorce action of his wife. Because he is a Christian, Ralph felt responsible to do everything he could to stop his wife from destroying their marriage. Time and again she rebuffed his suggestions for reconciliation. Even after she was excommunicated by their church, became pregnant by another man, and moved to another state, Ralph clung to the hope that she would return.

Much of Ralph's perseverance was commendable, but the sad fact was that he poured all of his time and energy into the dream of winning his wife back. He failed to take care of himself. He dropped out of all activities other than going to church and to work. He became obsessed with the idea that his wife would return. Meanwhile, his children laughed at him and his ex scorned him. It was not until his former spouse married another man that Ralph acknowledged that he could not have her back. Then he slowly began to regain a sense of balance in his life.

Why do we use denial? We are afraid of the future. We are afraid that we will lose control of our lives. And we are afraid of the intense feelings that may be unleashed if we honestly face the truth. But the facts must be faced and feelings must be experienced if we are to grow.

## Handling Denial

Denial can be overcome only by a gentle, yet firm confrontation with truth. An example of this took place recently in a small group in which I participated. A woman quietly asked her fellow group members, "Do you think that my husband may come back?"

An alumnus of the seminar responded. She said, "You know, I asked that same question. Well, he may come back . . . and he may not. But for the time being you will have to face things the way they are. I understand how you must feel. Let's talk about it after our session."

Over the years I have learned that one of the greatest benefits of a person's involvement in a divorce recovery program is the opportunity to talk with people who have faced the same experiences and walked down the same paths he is walking. Their counsel is seasoned with reality. Listening to

sensitive, experienced people is particularly helpful for someone in the initial shock of divorce. He
needs to be handled with care. And in a small
group he can learn about how others have learned
to cope. By observing the growth of others, he can
risk accepting the truth.

John has put it succinctly: "I didn't know that
anything was really wrong in my marriage. Her
leaving was like a bomb dropping on me. For a
time I couldn't do anything. But I guess that I
needed that time. The news of her leaving was like
getting hit with a pan of ice water. I needed some
time to get over the shock. And I needed to hear
from others who had been through it. Those were
the two things that helped me the most: time and
others who understood what I was going
through."

### Making the Transition: Denial to Anger

When denial is faced and reality is owned, the
"Oh, no—not me" of denial becomes, "Oh, yes—it
is me!" All of the emotions you have held back
through denial suddenly come rushing in. The response you have to all of these emotions is often
discovered in the next stage of the grief recovery
process. It is the time you dig into your resources
and pull out all of your ammunition. You use the
energy you have stored up to protect yourself
against the attack! Now is the time you turn to anger.

# CHAPTER SIX

# The Volcano Within
## (Anger)

You could see the shock on some of their faces. It happened during a small group session at a Fresh Start Seminar. The participants were sharing about the divorce experience and their feelings springing from that whirlwind of a crisis. Suddenly, one of the women let it all out. She said, "I was so angry at my husband for all that he did that I just wanted to kill him. So I took a contract out on his life. But I didn't have enough money to pay for it."

Somehow, even though the statement was so unexpected, each one in the small group was able to relate to this woman's feelings. All of them understood her because they, too, had felt the anger of divorce.

### The Anger of Divorce

The anger of divorce can break through at any time during marital disruption and litigation.

However, many people find that anger reaches its peak of intensity after they have experienced the futility of denial. Suddenly, all of the emotions that were resisted through denial break out! Feelings seem to explode! And when this happens, anything or anyone can be the target of that anger. God, friends, children, ex-spouse, parents, church, pets—virtually anything that gets in the way—can become the recipient of the explosive emotions. Of course, the focus of anger is usually the estranged spouse. And the legal process often centralizes anger on the issues of money and custody or visitation.

The anger of divorce can manifest itself in many ways. It can take active forms such as sarcasm, criticism, impatience, and even physical cruelty. For example, one man I know (a respected professional in his community) took the tires off his wife's car and dumped them at a garbage heap. I learned that one woman took the family dog to the veterinarian to be put to sleep because she didn't want her husband to keep the pet.

The anger of divorce can be expressed in passive, covert forms through stubbornness, restlessness, self-pity, nervousness, or withdrawal. Janice, a mild-mannered, well-educated professional woman, refused to sign her settlement papers. When questioned on this matter, she quietly said that her refusal to sign didn't have a thing to do with an attempt to keep her marriage together. No, she explained, she just wanted to prolong the divorce as long as possible because it irritated her husband!

The anger of divorce can be of such intensity and duration that many married people cannot understand it. Dr. Bruce Fisher, in his book *Rebuilding* (1981), tells the following story that demonstrates the uniqueness of divorce anger:

> In the *Des Moines Register* a true story appeared of a female who had been left by her husband. While driving by the park she saw her ex lying on a blanket with a girl friend. She drove into the park and ran over the former spouse and his girl friend with her car! Divorced persons respond to this story by exclaiming, "Right on! Did she back over them again?" Married people will gasp, "Ugh! How terrible!"

### Understanding the Anger of Divorce

Why is divorce anger so hostile and intense? Perhaps it is because anger is a response to relationships. One study has shown that close to 80 percent of anger is a response to the actions of other people rather than to circumstances or events (Collins, 1980).

I can understand this relational dynamic in anger. Prior to marriage, I thought that I had my anger feelings under control. I had even shared with people that since I became a Christian I no longer had anger problems. "God has resolved that issue in my life," I would say.

The truth is that while I was still single, I could control how vulnerable I would be toward others. If I didn't want others to get close to me, I could effectively close them out. If circumstances looked like they could end in a confrontation of anger, I would maneuver myself around them.

However, when I was married, I soon learned that all of my avoidance techniques would not work if I was serious about maintaining a healthy relationship with my wife. I also learned that my wife could push my anger buttons because she was so close to me. I was shaken—even overwhelmed at times—by my angry outbursts.

Anger is a relationship response. It is the opposite of indifference. We generally feel anger toward people who are important to us. We want their acceptance, approval, and affirmation. The fact that we feel any anger toward someone indicates a high level of involvement with that person. And when it comes to the anger of divorce, the feelings can be as intense as the intimacy that once characterized the marriage.

## The Character of Anger

Most of our beliefs about anger—and our experience of it—come from the training we received as children. Many of us grew up in families where we were led to believe it was always wrong to be angry. Others of us saw anger improperly handled, which translated into confusion, pain, and alienation in our households. So, whether we were told that anger was wrong or we were trained through the hard knocks of hurtful experience, most of us believe that it is wrong to be angry and that anger should be avoided at all costs.

Because most people think of anger in negative terms, they are often surprised to hear that the Bible doesn't confirm this conclusion. God's Word simply does not teach that anger is always wrong. For instance, Jesus felt significant anger toward the Pharisees and the money changers in the temple (Mark 11:15–17). Later, the apostle Paul taught, "Be angry, and do not sin" (Eph. 4:26).

In order to understand what the Bible does teach about anger, as well as to correct misunderstandings of this emotion, we need to make a clear distinction between anger feelings and anger expression. What we feel and what we do with those feelings are two separate issues. The truth is that everyone has anger feelings. They are God given. When we feel anger, we confirm that we are created in God's image. Pick up a Bible concordance and look up the word *anger*. You will discover that it is an important part of God's character.

We must learn that we are responsible for the ways we convey our anger. We are personally accountable for the ways we speak and act in response to our anger. Feelings and behavior are two different aspects of who we are. The feeling of anger can be expressed through many different behaviors. For example, a man I know vents his anger by beating up his own body. Another man I know often goes out and gets blind drunk. A third goes down to his basement and pounds nails into the wall. Still another cuts his grass every time he gets furious (and he has one of the best manicured lawns in town!).

### Managing Anger Feelings

Many people have said to me, "Look, I would love to control the expression of my feelings. And I have tried to control it, but I just can't do it."

One of my experiences helped me understand that anger feelings can be controlled. Our family was embroiled in what we call a "nuclear family reaction." Everyone was in the fray, including the dog. Suddenly, out of the blue, the telephone rang. There was dead silence. I went to the phone and answered it. I was quiet, gentle, and well-mannered. My family, in turn, was respectfully silent until the conversation was completed. Then, when the receiver went back on the hook, we were all back into the fight! None of us wanted this stranger to be aware of our family warfare. So we all pushed "pause" until it was "safe" to resume the battle.

I learned through that experience that we can

handle our anger feelings. The anger is not the problem. It is how we express it that counts. And we can learn how to manage our anger expressions.

Anger can actually become a helpful tool when it is handled properly. The key to anger management is learning how to use feelings for constructive purposes.

In his book *Anger: Yours and Mine and What To Do About It* (1981), Dr. Richard Walters suggests four methods we use to handle anger feelings. Two of them are negative, improper methods. Two of them are positive and helpful. I am going to modify these four methods to explore ways that the feelings of divorce can be handled in a beneficial manner.

*Rage*

The first negative method of coping with anger feelings is rage. Rage, which is sometimes called "catharsis," is the venting of anger on some object. It can be any object available or blamable at the time of the anger. Rage is the unleashing of emotional fury on a perceived enemy or the dumping of one's emotional load on a hapless victim.

In my mind's eye, I remember a scene from a sitcom. A psychiatrist is telling his patient, "I want you to go into your closet and let loose with a loud scream." Another time he says, "Go home to your bedroom and slug your pillow." Why does he make

these suggestions? The sitcom is parodying techniques that have often been used in actual therapy.
The purpose of this behavior is to vent angry feelings of rage without hurting anyone else.

Unfortunately, while these (or other) expressions of rage might make an individual feel better
for the moment, they do little to help one function
more productively. As a matter of fact, researchers
have shown that such behavior often increases aggressive behavior rather than decreases it.

In the Bible the idea of venting anger is never
suggested as a healthy form of anger management.
Just the opposite. Proverbs 29:11 states that "a
fool vents all his feelings." And current research
confirms this conclusion of Scripture. The
"energy" of anger must be rechanneled into positive forms of behavior.

### *Repression*

The second negative technique of anger management is repression. Repression is the quiet swal-
lowing of dissatisfaction. It is the stifling of anger
feelings. Since most of us are trained to think that
it is wrong to express anger feelings through rage,
we learn to close our mouths and hold our feelings
inside.

However, like a pressure cooker that tightly con-
tains the steam of boiling water, there is a great
deal taking place inside the body where anger feelings are being suppressed! The longer these anger

feelings are resisted, the more a "slush fund" of negative emotions is built up inside.

Sooner or later these feelings will come out. Perhaps this will happen through a serious physical problem such as a heart attack, a stroke, paralysis, or an ulcer. (John Powell has said, "When I repress my emotions my stomach keeps score.") Or repressed feelings emerge through a serious emotional problem such as depression, irritability, excessive fault finding, or hyperactivity. Repression is subtly reinforced by our society. Although outbursts of rage are unacceptable, it is okay to have something wrong with our bodies!

A casual friend of mine always seemed negative and critical. One day, while she was walking down the street, her legs suddenly collapsed beneath her. After extensive examinations, no physical symptoms for this sudden paralysis could be found.

Later, as we talked together, I learned about this woman's childhood. She was subtly trained to handle her feelings by repression. It became evident that there could be a direct link between her critical spirit, her paralysis, and the deep anger she had stored up for years. Through repression, she had become a walking emotional volcano! The "eruption" occurred as both an attitude problem and a physical problem.

I was recently sitting in a small group with a number of people. An older woman shared, "It wasn't until this evening that I realized that after

twenty-six years of marriage I had anger going
back to the second night of our marriage. I had
always stifled my feelings."

It is amazing how easy it is to repress our feelings of anger, and it is amazing how long we can
hold them inside without dealing with them. However, they will not simply go away, no matter how
much we wish they would. Something must be
done to resolve them.

### Resolution

Although we have all experienced them, rage
and repression are not healthy methods of anger
management. The last two methods utilize techniques that are more positive and healthy. The first
of these is resolution. Resolution means to openly
acknowledge that you are angry, but that you are
committed to honestly working through your feelings with the person(s) who has made you feel this
way. Resolution recognizes that anger is usually a
problem between persons. Therefore, when a person desires to resolve his anger, he takes this relational dynamic seriously. He goes to the person(s)
with whom he has a problem, and together they
confront the issues.

Because the goal of resolution is a restored relationship with the alienated person, this process requires two people who are willing to work with
each other until the problem is resolved and their
relationship is healed. Each person must acknowl-

edge offenses against the other. Each must ask for forgiveness. The result of such a process is often a deeper bond of friendship created through shared risk and mutual understanding.

Jerry's wife had attended a Fresh Start Seminar. Jerry was surprised at how the seminar seemed to help her cope with their separation. He learned from her that the seminar was to be held again in a nearby city. Motivated to see what would happen, Jerry took the time off to go to the seminar.

In his small group Jerry listened as others shared their experiences. Slowly throughout the weekend he began to realize how much pain he had caused his wife in their marriage. He came home and asked for her forgiveness. She, in turn, acknowledged her failures and sought his forgiveness. Today they are still reconciled.

Don't get the idea that everything is just "rosy" as a result of one weekend seminar! Jerry and his wife still have a great deal of work to do to rebuild a strong foundation for their marriage. However, the key is that they are working together and they are committed to maintaining openness and honesty with each other. This is what resolution is all about.

When the idea of resolution comes up, many divorced people just smirk. They think, *Hey, that is nice in theory. But it could never happen in my marriage! I tried to talk. I tried to relate with honesty. But he (or she) would never listen to me.*

Well, it is possible that resolution might not

work. After all, both partners must strive to bring about resolution. But many people write off the possibility of resolution because they assume it would not work, and they never attempt it. For such persons the real issue is not whether resolution will work. Rather, it is a question of courage. Do they have the courage to try it?

Many people would like to try resolution, but they do not know how to attempt it. To describe the steps toward resolution is beyond the scope of this chapter. However, one way to begin is to gain the support of a sensitive friend or counselor. Such a helper can aid you in thinking through what would be necessary to initiate resolution. The individual might also provide you with the encouragement to get started.

Resolution requires the commitment of both alienated partners if it is to succeed. And we must honestly recognize that resolution does not always work. A big question then becomes, "When resolution does not work, where can I turn? What can I do?"

## Redirection

When resolution does not work, you can apply the other positive method of anger management: redirection. Redirection is the decision to express anger's energy in an alternative but constructive manner. It is the commitment to take anger feelings and use them for positive good in the lives of others.

Redirection must be a conscious decision. You know that you are angry. You know that the person you feel angry toward will not work to resolve the problems with you. Therefore, you decide to take those feelings and use them as a positive investment in the lives of others.

An illustration of redirection is found in a fascinating story from the life of Jesus Christ. In Mark 3 we read that Jesus, moved by anger at the stubborn hearts of the religious leaders, healed a man with a shriveled hand. Jesus knew the religious leaders were not interested in reconciliation. They hated Him and wanted to kill Him. However, Jesus took His natural feelings of anger and channeled them into a constructive action that produced a positive result in the life of a hurting man.

Another example of redirection is evident in the Prison Fellowship. Prison Fellowship is an organization committed to working with prisoners and families of prisoners. Chuck Colson, the former aide to President Richard Nixon, started this organization as a result of his incarceration after the Watergate scandal. He has positively used the pain and hurt of his experience as the impetus to start a work that affects thousands of prisoners worldwide.

Whenever I go to a city to be involved in a Fresh Start Seminar, I am amazed at the fantastic commitment of the volunteers who help to run the program behind the scenes. As I talk to these volunteers, I hear the same comment over and over again: "When I attended Fresh Start, I was a wreck. During the seminar, I gained a sense of hope. I learned that my life could have a sense of purpose and direction. Maybe I couldn't get my marriage back together (even if I wanted to!), but I can help somebody else." This is redirection! Using anger feelings constructively. Redirecting these feelings, and gaining the satisfaction of being able to help others.

### Transition: Anger to Bargaining

It is a tremendous challenge to use anger in a constructive way. It takes practice and review. Even when you are working at it, you find that you can often move into the next stage on the slippery slope. It is the stage when you try to find an easy way to resolve all of the hassles and problems you have been facing in separation and divorce. You want to get it all over as quickly and as painlessly as possible. This stage is called "bargaining."

# CHAPTER SEVEN

# Microwave Solutions to Crockpot Problems
## *(Bargaining)*

The divorce papers were drawn up. At the last minute Pat's husband made a proposal that took her by surprise. He said that he would not sign the papers unless she gave him the first purchase option on their home whenever she would sell it. Furthermore, he wanted the agreement to state that he could purchase the home from Pat for the same price they had paid for it originally (about $60,000).

Pat had already been through much arguing and haggling over the settlement. She wanted to be finished with the whole mess and move on with her life. Under the circumstances, she felt that agreeing to this "little" thing would prevent further delay.

Years later, when Pat considered selling her home, she had a real estate agent estimate its market value. He told her that the home should sell for something in the neighborhood of $210,000! Pat learned the hard way that quick solutions can often cause big problems.

## The Dynamics of Bargaining

Bargaining can be explained as the attempt to find an easy solution to a complex problem. It is perhaps the most difficult stage to understand because it can take very complicated and intricate forms. For example, if past patterns of manipulation have proven effective in a marriage, it is likely that similar forms of bargaining will occur during marital separation. On the other hand, drastic changes in lifestyle and methods of communication might take place in bargaining.

Here are some examples of "deals" used in bargaining:

"I'll never work on the weekends again." "I will quit my bridge club."

"I'll take you out to dinner each week." "Let's go on that special vacation we have always dreamed about."

Bargaining can involve anything from a new hairstyle to more sexual activity to suggested outings. But the classic bargaining point when a marriage seems to be falling apart is: "I will go to a counselor."

Bargaining usually reflects the priorities or major concerns of a person. For example, Sam always thought in terms of money. So when the time came to work out a separation agreement with his wife, Sam already knew where he would place his emphasis. He prepared a very lucrative financial agreement for himself and then presented it to his wife saying, "Here, sign this and I won't contest your custody of the kids."

Bargaining is inevitably experienced by anyone going through a divorce. It can happen at any time during the divorce experience, but a predictable period of bargaining occurs when anger does not seem to be working. A partner reasons, "Since we are going to get a divorce, we might as well stop bickering and be mature about the whole thing." Unfortunately, this "maturity" often breaks down into selfish manipulation.

Dan was a Lutheran minister. Throughout their marriage, Dan's wife told him how much she hated being the wife of a pastor. She often shared how she wished he would get out of the ministry and enter a different profession.

However, Dan felt called to the pastorate and never seriously considered her request. He knew that they had marital problems, but he did not believe his pastoral role was a primary issue in their struggles. However, when his wife separated from him, Dan offered to leave the ministry if she would come back. He even sent her a copy of a resignation letter he had prepared to give to his congregation when she returned.

### Bargaining Versus Negotiation

Negotiation is often confused with bargaining.

However, negotiation and bargaining are not the same thing.

Negotiation is a normal part of healthy conflict. It takes place when two or more disputants come to mutual terms over matters of disagreement. In negotiation each participant is considered an equal. And each person recognizes that something will have to be given up in order to come to an agreement.

Bargaining is a power play. It is the attempt to gain desired ends by using any leverage that one might have available.

For example, Ed was divorced man, and he had no desire to remarry. He had been dating Janet for three years. Whenever Janet would bring up the topic of marriage, Ed would avoid the subject. Finally, Janet dropped Ed. It was only a few months later when Janet became engaged to another man. Ed was beside himself. He began to plot and dream of any possible way to stop Janet from marrying this other man. He cried. He argued. He bought her expensive jewelry. He would do anything to get her back—anything, of course, except consider marriage.

How does this story illustrate bargaining instead of negotiation? Ed used all the techniques and methods he knew to manipulate Janet into terminating her engagement. He wasn't talking with her in an open and honest manner. He wasn't respecting her as an equal. He didn't consider her feelings and concerns. Rather, he selfishly pushed his demands on her—albeit in subversive ways—to gain his own desired results. In a very real sense Janet's concerns meant nothing to him. The only thing that mattered was getting what he wanted. This is the power play of bargaining.

Another illustration of bargaining that is often seen in marriage and separation is the use of sex as a manipulative tool. For example, a partner might demand sexual acts many times a day. Then, when his spouse is unable or unwilling to meet his demands, he would make his partner feel inadequate.

Or consider the withholding of sex to force compliance or to punish undesirable behavior. Furthermore, think of the times when pregnancy or the threat of pregnancy is used as a bargaining tool.

Bargaining is not negotiation. It is the attempt to get what is desired by using any active or passive manipulation available.

## Why Do We Bargain?

Bargaining and manipulation seem to be ingrained in the human repertoire of methods we use to get what we want. And in our culture we expect to get what we want fast! After all, the problems we watch on television are resolved within thirty minutes or an hour. And we have learned to order our meals from a "fast-food" restaurant for the same reason.

*Therefore,* we say to ourselves, *there must be an easy and quick solution to this complex problem in our marriage.* So, we look for a microwave solution to our crockpot problems. Our marital problems do not spring up overnight. They are integrated into all of the history and shared experiences of the marriage. It took years for them to develop into a complicated and emotional rationale for divorce. They have been "simmering" in that crockpot for a long time.

As I stated earlier, many couples get counseling during this bargaining period. They want a "quick fix" to make their problems go away fast, fast, fast.

The Bridges are looking for that easy bargaining fix. They shared, "We separated after nine years of marriage. We have never spent one night apart these last nine years and now we are finding it harder to be separated than we ever expected."

Doris Bridges went on, "I left home because of my husband's frequent unemployment, alcohol abuse, and cocaine addiction. I figured we were bad for each other since we seem to feed into each others addictions. Since leaving, I've cleaned up my act. Now Mike wants me to come back. I know he has a long way to go, but I feel like I need him in my life again. Perhaps I can help him through his problems."

Mike explained, "Doris is right. I've been a bum. But now I know I can't go on alone. I told her if she will move back in, I'll stop the drugs and booze and get a job. This separation has made me realize how much I need her. I know when she comes back we will work it out together."

Can you catch the bargaining in their comments? They make promises and state their expectations, but Mike never demonstrated behavioral changes to validate any hope for a difference in their marriage. And neither Mike nor Doris established any goals or guidelines that could mark accountable growth. They just expected that things would work out after their reconciliation.

Doris moved back in with Mike, but soon they lapsed into the same destructive tendencies that caused the separation in the first place. The Bridges were trying to get it back together based on the assumption that everything would work out okay, even though nothing had worked out before.

The Bridges wanted to use an easy solution to a very complex problem. Without hard work and lifestyle changes, all the hope in the world would not resolve their difficulties. Healthy, long-term solutions take hours of honest negotiation; they require priority time in order to talk, change, review what has happened, and reorient expectations. Bargaining—finding an easy answer—will rarely produce the desired result.

### Poor Communication Patterns

If bargaining persists, future patterns of poor communication are often established. These bad habits can wrap an entire family up into years of extended arbitration and intense animosity.

The story of John Peters illustrates the damage that can occur in a family maintaining poor communication patterns. John grew up in a home where his father consistently used bargaining to get his own way. John's dad would regularly withhold affection from his children, and he would communicate with them only on his terms. He would parcel out his love as a reward for doing things his way. John even remembers how his father did not flinch at giving presents to one child while refusing to give them to others in order to show the "erring" children what it took to receive his love and care.

After the divorce of his parents, John continued to live with his father. Although the courts awarded ample time for John to spend with his mother, he rarely took advantage of seeing her. The reason was simple: his father made life so miserable after visitation that it wasn't worth the hassle and pain to see her. Furthermore, to avoid the constant harangues from her ex, John's mother stopped calling him. And since John was afraid to initiate contact with her, his mother assumed that he was disinterested in talking. Therefore, meaningful communication between mother and son ceased years ago.

Today, as a mature adult, John still feels that his mother could care less about him. And at the same time he carries a deep-seated anger toward his father for the way he was treated as a child. John is beginning to see some similar patterns of relating in his own marriage. And this scares him a great deal.

## Moving Beyond Bargaining

If we are to stop using the tools of bargaining, we must first recognize that all of us desire to have our own way. Let's face it. All of us have used manipulation and threats and promises to gain what we want. Here is the problem: we become so entrenched in these methods that we don't even know we are using them. And if we do recognize our bargaining patterns, we fail to understand how unhealthy they are to our relationships.

How can we break these habits and change our use of bargaining? We must evaluate our attitudes toward others as they are reflected in our methods of communication. We must ask ourselves questions like these:

- How do I feel toward this person?
- Do I want to understand his point of view or simply convince him of my ideas?
- Am I trying to get my own way, or am I sincerely interested in coming to a joint conclusion?
- Are my desired goals driving me to twist the truth or to shade it in ways that make my ideas look good?

• Am I anxious to get these issues resolved, or
am I willing to take as much time and invest as
much energy as needed to come to an honest conclusion?

Asking ourselves these kinds of questions is not
easy. They force us to stop and evaluate ourselves.
And they require us to acknowledge our motives
and dishonesty. However, they also expose the lies
of bargaining.

Once we can acknowledge that we are bargaining, we can refuse to play the game. We can choose
healthier communication patterns. We can be honest with ourselves and with those to whom we are
trying to communicate.

Growth through divorce requires a long-term rehabilitation, not a quick fix. It took years for your
marital problems to develop and compound. It
will take time and work to bring them to resolution.

### Making the Transition: Bargaining to Depression

You have seen that denial and anger will not resolve the problems of divorce. Neither will bargaining provide an easy solution to your complex
problems. At this point you might feel that your
back is against the wall. You have tried to maintain

control of your life and circumstances. But now you feel that you are losing control.

Instead of looking outside yourself, you begin to turn inward, asking a thousand questions that rarely have satisfactory answers. You become the brunt of all the hurt and pain. You become angry with yourself. You have come to the stage called "depression."

# CHAPTER EIGHT

# How Low Can I Go?
## (Depression)

She sat there silently as the others in her group shared their experiences of separation and divorce. When the opportunity came for her to contribute to the conversation, she looked down at the floor and shook her head. Yet as others opened up and expressed their feelings, she would look at them intensely, soaking in every word. At one point she mustered the courage to say something. But before a word could be spoken she burst into tears, unable to express what was going on inside her troubled heart. Many in the group assured her that they understood her dilemma. Each in a personal way expressed the message, "That's okay. You don't have to talk. We understand."

Depression. It has been defined in many ways. Some say it is like being in a black hole. Others say it is the feeling of being immobilized. Perhaps a Ziggy cartoon expresses it as well as anything else. The sun is shining all around, except on Ziggy. He has his own personal rain cloud pouring down on him wherever he goes. That is depression.

There is a natural stage of depression that everyone goes through when experiencing divorce. However, depression is a very complex state that extends beyond the circumstances of divorce. It can develop from many varied factors, such as one's physical condition, a bodily chemical imbalance, critical self-talk based on years of patterned low self-esteem, or circumstances that shatter one's life like a hammer blow. Someone going through a divorce should never assume that the marital situation is the only cause of depression. Yet it is good to remember that periods of depression are a normal part of the recovery process as one works toward adjustment.

Whenever anyone faces depression, it is beneficial to evaluate the factors that might be contributing to it. If you experience sustained depression for a period of three to four weeks, it can be quite helpful to seek support in working through this emotional challenge. A counselor, pastor, or personal physician can help you clarify the tangled issues creating the response of depression.

## The Depression of Divorce

Again, it must be emphasized that even if you have all the other areas of your life put together, you should expect a period of depression solely on the basis of the disruption of your marriage. Although the characteristics of this emotional "down time" can be complex and varied, I want to explore a few of the more common ones.

The first characteristic is sadness. You feel low in spirit, hopeless, and helpless. There seems to be a sense of darkness in your life. One person shared, "Oh, I never thought that I would become one of those divorce statistics!" Another stated, "Everything I have tried has failed. I lost my home, my family, and my friends. Why should I keep on trying?"

Along with sadness comes the tendency to withdraw. One of my friends put it very simply. He said, "Look, I can't take the chance of being hurt again. I'm just going to keep everything to myself. I'll go to work, come home and go to bed. I don't trust anyone anymore."

A woman at a seminar shared her desire to withdraw in this way: "No one would want to be with me. If I couldn't please my husband, I can't please anyone."

A second characteristic of divorce depression is a pessimistic attitude. You find that you begin to apply the negative consequences of divorce to every aspect of life. This pessimism is often conveyed through statements such as these:

"I'm going to be divorced forever" (as if divorce is some sort of incurable disease).

"No one appreciates me or understands me" (and because I've withdrawn, I won't take the risk to see if people would extend themselves to me).

"All men are rotten" (or vice versa!).

"I've failed at the most important relationship in my life; therefore, I am a failure" (even if there are facts that disprove this statement).

As you withdraw more and more from others, you deepen your sense of sadness and pessimism. The results of such a pattern are found in three more characteristics of divorce depression.

One of these is a refusal to pay attention to personal health and appearance. Many in depression let their bodies go to pieces. I have a friend who forgot about a balanced lifestyle and would work fourteen to sixteen hours a day, seven days a week. Another person I know went for days on a diet that consisted only of thin mint cookies.

Depression can also alter appearance. One woman refused to get dressed for days on end. A man I know sports a very nicely trimmed beard. You can imagine how surprised I was to learn that he grew it while in depression over his divorce. It wasn't planned. He just went so long without shaving that he found himself with a beard!

Another characteristic is the failure to invest any energy in things that create a sense of personal enjoyment and fulfillment, such as hobbies, projects around the home, or volunteer organizations. Consider what happened to Sue as an example of this neglect. There was a time when she experienced great enjoyment by singing in the church choir. When her husband left her, Sue withdrew from everything, including her singing commitments. She lost the companionship of many with whom she sang, and she also lost that valuable sense of meaning that she found in the use of her musical talents.

The final characteristic of divorce depression is loneliness. You feel abandoned by others. Often you feel as though you have lost membership in what had once been a secure social network. If you have felt this, you probably relate to Joyce, who shared, "More than anything else I wanted my marriage to work. If I couldn't keep that together, I'm sure that no one would ever want to spend time with me. Everyone must view me as a loser."

Loneliness is often the result of a cycle of rejection and withdrawal. The low self-image that comes from the impact of divorce causes you to fear approaching others. At the same time friends, family, and other acquaintances do not know what to say to you. Therefore, they leave you alone. As a response to this combination of problems, you don't exert the energy to meet new people. You don't socialize even when you go out. So you feel even more rejection, which feeds on your low self-image. The problem perpetuates itself.

When you are at the bottom of the slippery slope, in the pit of depression, you even feel rejected by God. You probably relate to the cry of the psalmist when he shared from his weeping heart: "Why do You stand afar off, O LORD? Why do You hide in times of trouble?" (Ps. 10:1).

### Coping with the Depression of Divorce

It is critical for anyone facing the depression of divorce to recognize that depression is not necessarily a sign of personal or spiritual weakness. You only have to study the personalities of key figures in the Bible to learn that depression can be a very natural and normal experience.

For example, Elijah was an outstanding Old Testament prophet. Yet after his greatest success, he sank into a deep depression. He even reached the point of praying that he might die: "It is enough! Now, LORD, take my life, for I am no better than my fathers!" (1 Kings 19:4).

As you continue to read Elijah's story, you will see that God never condemned or criticized His prophet. Rather, He provided the opportunity for Elijah to recover from depression by giving him proper nourishment and rest.

Another significant biblical figure who faced intense depression was the apostle Paul. Read where he shared with his friends at Corinth about this experience: "We do not want you to be ignorant, brethren, of our trouble which came to us in Asia: that we were burdened beyond measure, above strength, so that we despaired even of life. Yes, we had the sentence of death in ourselves" (2 Cor. 1:8–9).

Because we find that godly people of the Bible experienced depression, we must conclude that it is not necessarily unusual or unspiritual. It is a natural reaction to negative experiences and events. And it is part of our God-given emotional system. Since our bodies can handle only a certain level of stress and conflict, depression acts like a circuit breaker in an electrical system. When a dangerous overload hits, the breaker clicks off the power to protect the system. Similarly, when we face an emotional overload, the breaker of depression clicks off to restore emotional energy and help us to cope.

## The Needs of the Depressed

When you are experiencing the pain of depression, you have several essential needs. First, like Elijah, you need to have enough rest and nourishment. It is not unusual for someone in depression to eat poorly. Junk foods full of salts, sugars, and fats do not provide the nutrients required for your body to handle the added stress. And if you are depressed, you may tend to stay up late at night. Often single parents find themselves in this trap. Pushed and pulled by the activities of the day, they overextend those precious evening hours that they have to themselves. However, the depressed condition is intensified by exhaustion. Therefore, the discipline to rest, as well as to eat properly, is vital in coping with depression.

A second need is to understand that God is truly

in control of the situation. Recently, I have been
impressed with the biblical character Joseph. He
withstood adversities that could have sent anyone
into a depressive tailspin. It started when his jeal-
ous brothers sold him as a slave into Egypt. Then,
he was unjustly framed and sent to prison where
he remained for over ten years. Finally, after a
unique set of events, Joseph became a leader in the
Egyptian government and the director of national
famine relief.

In retrospect, when he evaluated all that had
taken place, Joseph commented to his brothers
(whom he had saved from the famine), "You mean
evil against me; but God meant it for good" (Gen.
50:20). Imagine looking back on the pain and injus-
tice he had suffered, yet acknowledging the control of God over all of it!

When I shared this story with a friend who has
suffered numerous depressive attacks, he said,
"Sure, Joseph could affirm God's control. He saw
how it all turned out."

My friend's comment forced me to review Joseph's life. I discovered that Joseph consistently
affirmed God's control, and his own responsibility
to submit to that control, throughout his difficult
experiences. It wasn't just in the easy times that
Joseph affirmed God's caring hand. It was in the
deepest times of difficulty that he confessed it!

Every person struggling through depression
ought to spend some time thinking through Psalm
73. This psalm records the journey of a man

named Asaph from a point of depression to an affirmation of faith. He learned that he could affirm God's control in the midst of the mess. Better than that, this affirmation of God's care gave him hope in the mess! Take a moment to read a few verses from his psalm:

> Thus my heart was grieved,
> And I was vexed in my mind.
> I was so foolish and ignorant;
> I was like a beast before You.
> Nevertheless I am continually with
>     You;
> You hold me by my right hand.
> You will guide me with Your counsel,
> And afterward receive me to glory.
>
> Whom have I in heaven but You?
> And there is none upon earth that I
>     desire besides You.
> My flesh and my heart fail;
> But God is the strength of my heart
>     and my portion forever (vv. 21–26).

Third, if you are dealing with divorce depression, you need to be appreciated. As we have seen, it is easy to sink into feelings of rejection and self-pity and to avoid people when depressed. It takes energy and determination to break out of this cycle. Appreciation comes, as often as not, when you take the time to serve others.

For some, service to others comes from continuing to perform unavoidable responsibilities. Taking care of children might be the thing that forces certain individuals to get out of themselves. Or friends who will not allow a relationship to cease can make persons feel appreciated. However, at times it simply takes raw determination to break through fears and find a way to share with others.

Dr. Karl Menninger, the famous psychiatrist, had just finished a lecture on depression, and he was answering questions from the audience. "What would you advise a person to do," asked one, "if that person felt deeply depressed to the point of having a nervous breakdown?"

To the group's astonishment, Dr. Menninger replied, "Lock up your house, go across the railroad tracks, find someone in need, and do something to help that person."

Rev. Hosea Williams is a black leader in Atlanta, Georgia. Every year he sponsors a Christmas dinner for the poor. He enlists people throughout the city to serve the poor on Christmas Day. Last year, a few days after the holiday, an affluent woman saw Rev. Williams in a large department store. She came over to him and gave him a big hug. While he was still recovering from shock, the woman said that she was a widow of many years. She shared how much she hated the holiday season because of the deep loneliness she felt. However, on Christmas morning she heard about the dinner for the poor. On a whim she decided to help. Then she explained, "For the first time in years, I felt the joy of giving to someone else. And I haven't felt that good in a long time! This Christmas hasn't been depressing; it has been wonderful!"

You can catch some of the dynamic of service in the words of Jesus when He said, "For whoever desires to save his life will lose it, but whoever loses his life for My sake will save it. For what profit is it to a man if he gains the whole world, and is himself destroyed or lost?" (Luke 9:24–25).

There are three other things you should do as you work at coping with the depression of divorce. One of these is to honestly face how you feel toward yourself. Sometimes depression is defined as anger that has turned inward. Listen to the way that you talk to yourself. Examine the attitudes that you have about your work, your looks, your character, and your relationships.

The second thing you need to do is to forgive yourself. In the chapter on anger we considered how difficult it would be to come to resolution with your ex-spouse. However, an even greater challenge is to come to the point of resolution with yourself! I have found that the best way to learn self-forgiveness is to review the fact that God has forgiven me.

In Matthew 18, Jesus tells a fascinating parable of a king who forgave a man the debt of several million dollars. After this man was forgiven, he went to a friend and demanded payment on a note of only a few dollars. When his debtor could not pay, the man who had been forgiven millions threw his friend into the debtors' prison. When the king heard of this ingratitude, he reversed his decision and threw the unforgiving man into prison.

The point of the story is obvious but full of truth. If we have truly been forgiven by God, it is the height of impertinence for us to refuse forgiveness to others. Yet we often fail to place ourselves in the category of those we need to forgive. Of course, if we have not experienced the forgiveness of God, it is understandable why self-forgiveness would be difficult. But if we have understood and experienced the cleansing power of God to forgive, we must forgive ourselves. This is critical to successfully handling the depression of divorce.

The final thing you must do to cope with divorce depression is to associate with others who comprehend the difficulty of your experience. It is hard for people who have not been through a divorce to understand what you are experiencing. Persons who have not had to face the challenge of personal depression may be able to sympathize, but not empathize, with your feelings. You need to find a few friends who will invest the time and energy—and have the understanding and experience—to listen to you. You need helpful insights from those who have walked down the same paths that you are walking.

One of the most encouraging experiences for individuals who attend a Fresh Start Seminar (or other divorce recovery programs) is being able to share with people who understand. The small group sharing times are always the most popular aspect of our program. In these sessions, people learn that they are no longer outsiders. For once they feel that they belong. And what a joy to discover people who have survived the whirlwind! Their example can show that there is hope after all!

## Making the Transition: Depression to Acceptance

The interesting thing about depression is that although you feel you are at the bottom of the pit, the fact that you have reached depression means you are moving closer to acceptance. Depression is often a sign that you have come to grips with the reality of your situation. Instead of playing games, you are taking personal responsibility for your life. Yes, that can be depressing because you must look hard at all of your losses. And you must face the challenge of your future. This isn't pleasant, but it is reality.

You must hit bottom before you can look up. By reviewing your present condition with honesty, you can take the steps necessary to move on with your life. Denial, anger, and bargaining didn't work. Now, while in depression, you are willing to do whatever it takes to be healed. Therefore, you are closer to acceptance than you could have imagined. Acceptance is not reaching some euphoric level of joy. Nor is it the return to things "as they were" before the pain. Rather, acceptance is coming to the steady state of incorporating all of your divorce experience into your personal history. And with that honest acceptance, you can get on with your life.

# CHAPTER NINE

# Redefining Normal
## (Acceptance)

The ancient city of Jerusalem was a city of many gates. One of these gates, called Bethesda (the Sheep Gate), was a site where many disabled people gathered. Their reason for making this a gathering point was the special pool located at Bethesda. They were convinced that miraculous healings took place at this pool.

Once, when coming up to Jerusalem, Jesus spent some time with the invalids at the pool of Bethesda. Scripture records the conversation He had with one man who had been waiting by the pool for thirty-eight years (John 5:2–9). The keynote of the conversation came when Jesus asked this man a most penetrating question: "Do you want to be made well?"

Can you imagine asking a man who had been waiting thirty-eight years for a healing, one who seemed to have no other recourse than the slim expectation of a miracle, if he wants to be healed? At first such a question seems preposterous!

But Jesus understood human nature much better than we do. Ask a nurse in a rehabilitation hospital if she understands the point of Jesus'
question. She would immediately know why Jesus
asked it. She probably has seen hundreds of disabled people who have given up hope for healing.
Perhaps they have even given up hope for life. She
would know that some invalids would rather remain crippled than go through the discipline of
convalescence.

## Acceptance Versus Resignation

The person who has given up hope for healing
has given in to resignation. Resignation is the passive, gloomy attitude that combines the feelings of
failure with a refusal to do anything about one's
problems. It is summed up in a little jingle I
learned in childhood:

> Nobody likes me,
> everybody hates me,
> let's go eat some worms.

When I think of resignation, I am reminded of a
man named Peter. The first time he attended our
seminar he lasted only one night. Upon returning
to the seminar a year and a half later, he acknowledged that he attended the first time only because
his mother had prepaid his registration. Furthermore, she literally drove him up to the door of the

sponsoring church! He shared, "I had given up on my family, on other people, and on God. I just wanted to be left alone. I remained in deep depression for well over a year."

Resignation doesn't always take the form of extended withdrawal and depression. Sometimes it reveals itself as deep-seated bitterness. Whatever form it takes, resignation is nothing like acceptance.

Acceptance is the active, creative willingness to acknowledge the limitations of a difficult condition. Furthermore, a person in acceptance is willing to take the limitations and use them for his benefit. Acceptance is coming to terms with a problem and then continuing to grow, refusing to be preoccupied with the past (Tournier, 1957).

At a meeting of Alcoholics Anonymous, a long-time participant shared how she grew up in a very abusive home. As a result of her childhood, this woman found that she had acquired few of the skills needed to cultivate friendships. She received emotional rewards by doing better than other people in as many areas of life as possible. It took years of hard work for her to discover that this hypercompetitiveness came from her dysfunctional background. Now she is learning how to use her competitive spirit in a positive way. She no longer compares herself to others or attempts to "beat" them out. Rather, she seeks to accomplish constructive goals and help her associates to succeed. She is discovering what it means to translate limitations into positive benefits.

Acceptance is the attitude portrayed by Jesus Christ in the Garden of Gethsemane when He prayed, "Now My soul is troubled, and what shall I say, 'Father, save Me from this hour'? But for this purpose I came to this hour. Father, glorify Your name" (John 12:27–28).

Not long ago I was in Washington, D.C., for a seminar. The first night, I saw a woman who had been in my small group a year earlier. She shared, "Do you remember me from the last seminar? I cried through the whole thing." This time she was a small group leader! She went on, "I finally realized that no one was going to come along and fix me. I decided to take my life in hand and start making some changes. Slowly I took more chances. I began to feel better about myself. I found that I wasn't as self-conscious in social situations. Eventually, I began to realize that I was making plans and actually feeling fulfillment in my new lifestyle."

## Characteristics of Acceptance

Acceptance won't just "happen." You don't wake up one morning and find yourself in acceptance. Like the other stages, it is a phase you grow into over a period of time. However, unlike the other stages, acceptance is an entrance to a new beginning: the beginning of a fulfilled life as a single-again adult.

Perhaps it is the fact that acceptance means a new beginning in life that makes it so desirable for those who are going through divorce. Time after time when I explain the stages of divorce and recovery to people, they respond by saying that they are already in acceptance. They say this because they truly want to be in acceptance. And they confuse the idea of acceptance with the fact that they accept the reality of their divorce. However, acceptance is not simply the willingness to live with the fact that you are divorced. Acceptance means coming to the point that the implications of your divorce are not dominating your life. It takes much longer to get to this stage than you want to believe or acknowledge.

I think of Sandy, a woman in a small group I led a few years ago. Her husband had suddenly left her for a female associate at work. Though this had happened only a few months earlier, Sandy shared with the group, "I still don't understand why John left me, but I have come to accept that I shouldn't expect him back unless the Lord does a miracle. It is hard to explain. I still love John, but I'm willing to lose him if that's the Lord's will. I guess I have just been given peace about the whole thing."

Sandy thought she was in acceptance. It was futile for any of us to gently explain that she still had a great deal of grief work ahead. She wouldn't hear it!

Sandy came back to the next seminar held in

her city. When I talked with her, she shared that
things had really changed! She said, "Oh boy, was
I naive the last time I was here! I guess that is what
you called denial, huh? Well, I am mad at John
now, really mad—and I also feel kind of stupid that
I made everything sound so sweet before. The Lord
is really helping me through this mess, but I
haven't arrived yet!"

At that time Sandy was serving as a small group
leader at the seminar. And she was extremely effective in this role because she could honestly
share what she had been through and how she felt
at the moment.

How, then, do you understand if you are in acceptance? I have found six characteristics that
stand out as landmarks on the road to acceptance.
None of them signify that you have "made it" to
this stage. But each is a marker of encouragement
that you are in the process of moving toward acceptance. Like the signs on a highway stating that
you are coming closer to your destination, the experience of each characteristic says that you are
coming nearer to acceptance.

### Characteristic #1—Recognizing Your Marriage Is Over and Your Divorce Is Complete

This characteristic emphasizes that you are no
longer expecting or yearning for your marriage to

come back together. It does not mean you are closed to the possibility of reconciliation. It does mean that you are not looking toward reconciliation as your only hope and expectation. Rather, you openly acknowledge that you are divorced and no longer married. It also means you understand that it is useless to continue arguments and disputes over who was "right" or "wrong." The time has come to move on with your life and goals. Now you are basing your expectations on the realities of the present, not the dreams of the past or the hopes of some fantasized future.

A few years ago there was a television special entitled "Divorce Wars." One of the key lines came toward the end of the show when an experienced domestic attorney wisely said to his client, "There are no winners in an adversarial divorce. Both sides lose. The only winner [in divorce] is the one who stops fighting."

Ann was divorced about three years ago. She marks the turning point in her growth as a time when she was feeling a great deal of anger: anger toward her former spouse, anger toward her parents, and anger toward herself. It was on a Saturday night. The kids were in bed. Ann took the few precious hours of quiet to muse over her circumstances. The more she thought, the angrier she became. While sitting in the bathroom crying, she looked up and saw herself in the mirror. Then she started to talk to herself. She said, "Hey, isn't it about time you stop thinking about what might have been, and what David has done to you? It's time you start to take care of yourself!"

Of course, there was nothing wrong with the grief Ann was expressing in her tears. However, she came to a point of honest recognition that the past was complete. That recognition started her on the path to acceptance.

### Characteristic #2—Being Honest with Yourself and Your Feelings

The truth is that we are often the most dishonest with ourselves. We make up all kinds of excuses for the way we act. At the same time, we deny the churning that we feel inside while we exert all our energy maintaining the facade that we "have it all together." However, when we are willing to lay our fears and anxieties out on the table and face them, we are on the way toward acceptance.

Let me give you an example. I shared earlier that full recovery from divorce takes much more time than most people want to think or believe. Dr. Robert Weiss of Harvard University estimates that it takes "from two to four years [for recovery] with the average being closer to four than two." Similarly, Dr. Judith Wallerstein (1989) has made these important observations from her fifteen-year study of divorced families:

> We have found that it takes women an average of three to three and one-half years and men two to

two and one-half years to reestablish a sense of external order after the separation.

Getting one's external life back on track, however, does not begin to resolve the profound internal changes that people experience in the wake of divorce. . . . The postdivorce family and the remarried family are radically different from the original intact family. Relationships are different. Problems, satisfactions, vulnerabilities, and strengths are different. People may get their lives back on track, but for most the track runs a wholly different course than the one they were on before divorce.

Divorce is deceptive. Legally it is a single event, but psychologically it is a chain—sometimes a never-ending chain—of events, relocations, and radically shifting relationships strung through time, a process that forever changes the lives of the people involved.

Based on this research, one aspect of honesty with yourself and your feelings is that you understand that your recovery will take some time. Instead of trying to rush the process, or circumvent the experience, you openly confess that you are on the road to acceptance. Further, you allow yourself the freedom of *not* "arriving" as yet!

Dianne has been divorced for four years. She shared recently that she had a funny experience talking with a friend about her divorce. She explained, "A woman told me that she was often feeling suicidal about the whole experience of her divorce. I told her that I once felt the same way. I

said, 'You'll get over it! I don't feel suicidal anymore; now I feel homicidal!'"

Dianne is able to be honest—and humorous—
about her feelings. Furthermore, she knows that
she is progressing along the road to recovery. She
added, "I have been keeping a journal about the
whole mess. I was able to share a few paragraphs
with my friend who was feeling suicidal. She was
really encouraged to know that someone else had
been down the same paths."

### Characteristic #3—Establishing and Maintaining Friendships

In her study on death and dying, Dr. Elisabeth
Kübler-Ross learned that patients move with
greater ease through the stages of death, first,
when they are loved enough by a significant person that they can accept themselves, and second,
when they share their feelings with this person.

The development of healthy, balanced friendships is critical in the process of divorce recovery.
And this is not necessarily an easy thing to do.
Many persons have found that their best friends
seem to abandon them while they are going
through the divorce. Others discover that those
with whom they used to be close simply do not understand what they are going through. Or worse
than that, their friends don't want to invest the
time and energy to understand the divorce.

Furthermore, the challenge of developing significant friendships is made more difficult by your reluctance to let others get close to you. One friend explained this to me in a graphic way: "Making friends after your divorce is like going to the dentist. Your need for friendships is as real as the pain of an abscess in your tooth. You go to that dentist, but you don't want him to touch your mouth! It hurts too much. Friendships are like that. You want to get to know a few people, and you want to share your experiences with them. But you don't want them to get too close. You are afraid of the pain. It can hurt too much."

When you are able to be close to a few others, you have made a significant step toward acceptance. The acceptance that you find in others can help you accept yourself and your circumstances.

And by the way, although this point is controversial, I am convinced that the best friendships you can develop in the recovery process are those with members of the same sex. Now, don't get me wrong. I am not saying that good, honest, and wholesome friendships can't (or shouldn't) be made with those of the opposite sex. However, what I mean is that friends of the same sex take away the threat of emotional entanglement. There are times when you can't handle the "otherliness" of the opposite sex. You need friends, but friends who are like you, friends who are safe. You need a few intimate friends with whom you can stop playing games and share what is really going on inside. And after a divorce, many people find this kind of intimacy too difficult—or threatening—with a person of the opposite sex.

Another realistic problem of deep friendships with the opposite sex during recovery is the possibility that you or your friend may misinterpret the intentions or expectations of the relationship. This can lead to fantasizing about the "potential" of remarriage or to coping with postdivorce promiscuity, which is so prevalent among those reentering the single life. Many books on divorce recovery portray postdivorce sex as a normal, healthy part of getting your life back together, but nothing can be further from the truth. Sexual liaisons and affairs can send you head over heels back down the slippery slope. It is bad enough to go through one major disappointment with the opposite sex. But the sex trap can set you up for betrayal and faithlessness again and again.

Divorce recovery needs to be a time of regathering strength. Honest friendships bring significant stability. You need to focus on relationships that will build you up, not bring you down.

### Characteristic #4—Learning to Control Your Thought Life

Probably one of the greatest challenges you face in divorce recovery is the discipline of your mind. You will find yourself reviewing and fantasizing the past. The only thing that will snap you out of these unhealthy thoughts is to rigorously confront them with the hard truth of reality.

This problem of re-creating the past in the mind and living in the dream world of what was or what might have been is not limited to those going through divorce. I am reminded of the emphasis that the Bible places on the discipline of the mind. The apostle Peter urged his readers to "prepare your minds for action" (1 Pet. 1:13). To the Christians in Corinth, Paul explained, "[We take] captive every thought to make it obedient to Christ" (2 Cor. 10:5 NIV).

How can you learn to control your mind? Well, at first this might seem too simple for you, but the discipline of the mind begins by understanding what you are thinking. Only when you know what you are thinking can you replace your thoughts with healthy and encouraging topics. You should take some time every day to review what you have been thinking. Write these thoughts and subjects down. Critique yourself. Ask yourself questions such as, "Is this subject going to help me?" and "Is this encouraging my growth and recovery?" Be particularly aware of your self-criticism. Are you being realistic with yourself? Or do you find yourself restating negative comments that significant people have said to you in the past?

Norman Wright has suggested a very simple technique that many people have found helpful in the discipline of their minds. He calls it "the

STOP/THINK method." Take an index card and write the following verse on it:

> Finally, brethren, whatever things are true, what-ever things are noble, whatever things are just, whatever things are pure, whatever things are lovely, whatever things are of good report, if there is any virtue and if there is anything praiseworthy—meditate on these things (Phil. 4:8).

On the other side of the card write STOP. When you catch yourself in a negative frame of mind, pull out the card and say to yourself (aloud if possible), "STOP!" Then turn the card over and repeat Philippians 4:8.

By learning how to control your thought life, you are taking significant responsibility for yourself. Not just for what you are doing with your time, but more important, for what you are doing with your mind. And that is an important step in the acceptance process.

### Characteristic #5—Looking Forward, Not Backward

This characteristic means that acceptance is oriented toward the future rather than the past. It is a partner with the idea of disciplining your thought life. Looking forward means that you focus your mind on what is happening, or can happen, rather than on what has happened.

Let me give you an example. One of the struggles during separation and divorce is a preoccupation with the former spouse. Whether the thoughts are positive or negative, they are still there. Perhaps one individual wishes he would come home. Or maybe another blames every bad thing that happens on the fact that "she left me." Regardless of the circumstances, the mind comes back to thoughts of the ex like a yo-yo that returns to the hand of the one using it.

Coming to acceptance means that you are occupied less and less by thoughts of your former marriage partner. This does not mean that you deny the importance of that part of your personal history. But it is history. Now you are moving on with life.

The other day a friend surprised me with this candid remark. He said, "I was fixing breakfast. And my toaster must have blown a fuse or something because there were a few sparks and a little cloud. The toaster was shot. Now, do you know what I said as I picked up the toaster and threw it into the trash, even though this is four years after my divorce? I said, 'It's Karen's fault!' Then I stopped and considered what I had just yelled out. I haven't lived with that woman for four years. I haven't even thought of her very much since last Christmas. I didn't even own this toaster when we were married. And here I am blaming her for its breaking!"

Then my friend concluded, "Do you want to

know the really encouraging thing I learned
through that incident? I learned that I hadn't been
thinking of her very much. I used to blame all of
my problems on Karen. That was the first time I
had said such a thing for months!"

Another aspect of looking forward is accepting
responsibility for the things you contributed to
your divorce. Until you understand the mistakes
you made in your marriage and you have taken
steps to correct them, you will not be in a position
to grow in the future. These unresolved issues and
personal weaknesses will keep you from progressing in maturity as well as in the ability to develop
strong friendships.

For many people, it is difficult to face the fact
that they contributed to the demise of their marriage. A way to come to grips with this fact is to
view your former marriage like a doubles tennis
match. One partner might have been responsible
for a greater number of misses and faults. Either
partner might have played the final shot that cost
the match. However, both partners contributed to
the loss and both experienced defeat. You never
beat your own partner.

Dr. Joseph Frederico (1979) expands on this idea
of accepting personal responsibility when he
states,

> Both persons in a divorce must accept responsibil-
> ity for the marital failure. . . . the dissolution of a
> marriage is an extended process involving a long

series of actions and reactions. The desire to see a divorce in terms of pure guilt and pure innocence contradicts interpersonal realities.

The apostle Paul knew what it meant to resolve the past and set his eyes on his present responsibilities and future opportunities. In a context where he recounts past experiences, Paul shifts from thinking on the past to focusing on the future. He explains,

> But one thing I do, forgetting those things which are behind and reaching forward to those things which are ahead, I press toward the goal for the prize of the upward call of God in Christ Jesus (Phil. 3:13–14).

### *Characteristic #6—Developing a New Source of Hope*

It is normal and natural for two people to base many of their personal hopes and dreams on their marriage. When a marriage falls apart, partners quickly discover that they were building expectations on a frail foundation. Of course the discovery that marriage is not a strong basis for ultimate fulfillment is not limited to those going through divorce. Each day widows and widowers are faced with the blunt fact that life must go on beyond marriage.

When your marriage crumbles, you fall back on your belief system for security and hope. Therefore, what you believe about this world, about life, and about eternal life is critical. One person stated this in the following manner:

> It isn't what happens to a person so much as how he reacts to what happens to him that makes a difference; and how he reacts will be determined by his inner resources of heart and mind . . . that is, by what he really believes.

Each of us has a belief system. Perhaps the majority of our convictions are subconscious. However, the stress of a crisis will force us to draw upon all of our inner resources. At this time the strength and the validity of our beliefs are tested. The upheaval of divorce does this to us. We are forced to examine what we really believe and depend upon. We are required to consider the basis for hope in our lives.

Each of us must answer this question about hope. Do we have a source of meaning and purpose that can stand solidly when everything in this world seems to be crumbling around us? If we have no basis of hope beyond the fragile components of our personal lives, what do we have to live for?

These questions ultimately bring us to the issue of faith. Faith is simply the expectations we hold as our basis for living. It goes beyond the level of our feelings to the arena of our expectations. Dr. Paul Tournier affirms this when he explains,

"However difficult the tangle of psychological reactions, it seems obvious to me that religious faith
is the most powerful source of real acceptance."

## Transition: Acceptance to Hope

Perhaps your whirlwind of separation and divorce has driven you to review your sense of hope.
Maybe you have been examining what you really
believe. And you are wondering how God feels
about you and your divorce. We shall spend some
time looking into these questions in the next chapter.

# CHAPTER TEN

# How Does God Feel About Me?

My friend Bill was an executive in a large national corporation. One of his many responsibilities was to keep an eye out for qualified men and women to move up the ladder of the organization. Bill would track the progress of these people in order to maintain a high quality of developing leadership.

Bill was particularly impressed with John, who was in one of the field offices. Bill thought that John had a great deal of potential. However, John faced a significant problem: his daughter was suffering from leukemia. Therefore, to help John, Bill transferred him from the field to corporate headquarters located in a city with a hospital specializing in the treatment of leukemia. Bill hoped this transfer would provide helpful training for John as well as offer the type of medical treatments that his daughter would never receive in their present location.

John performed very well in his new job. Unfortunately, things did not go so well with his daughter's treatment. Within two years she'd passed away.

In the midst of the family's natural grieving for the girl, Bill transferred John to the field office located in his hometown. John's family was able to go through this time of difficulty and transition near relatives and friends.

A few years later Bill brought John back to the corporate office. Not long after John's return, a new president was appointed for the corporation. The new president began to gather younger men around himself as his advisers. At the same time, older men who had been in leadership began to be excluded from key strategy sessions. Finally, one after another, the older men were terminated from employment. My friend Bill was laid off. You can imagine how he felt when he learned that John had recommended his termination.

We can all understand Bill's anger and bitterness. After all, there is no pain that strikes the core of the soul like the rejection of a friend.

Consider this question. After experiencing such a devastating blow from a man he had so greatly helped, what would it take for Bill to be reconciled to John? What would need to occur so that Bill could trust John once again?

If you have been through separation and divorce, you probably understand the difficulty of reconciling Bill and John. Few people in the world are better prepared to understand the cost of reconciling two alienated people than those who have gone through the termination of a marriage. If you have muddled through the slippery slope of divorce recovery, you know that reconciliation takes more than moving back into the same house (if married) or mumbling some sort of apology.

### Pam's Story

Pam was married for about fifteen years. She and her husband had two children. In the last two years of their marriage, Pam's husband began to live with another woman. He didn't divorce Pam. He simply lived with his girlfriend. He would come back to Pam and the kids over the weekend, then return to his girlfriend's apartment during the week.

How long would you tolerate such an arrangement? Pam put up with it for about two years. Finally, out of frustration, she asked me what she could do about the situation. She said, "I am really confused. My husband says that he wants to live with me, he wants the marriage, and he wants to be a good father for our children. But he keeps acting like he won't change."

As we talked, Pam and I isolated at least three things that would have to take place if her marriage was to continue. First, Pam felt her husband would have to own up to the fact that he was doing something wrong. As simple as this acknowledgment of wrong behavior might seem, it is difficult for men and women to express. People have often said to me, "I know that you and others think what I am doing is wrong. Well, it may be wrong. But I am going to keep doing it, and I don't care what you or my friends or God thinks about me. I am going to do what I want to do." Others might say, "What right do you have to tell me what I am doing is wrong?"

It is important to point out here that we have our own ideas of right and wrong. And we have our own ideas about God.

For the general populace to pool opinions on God or right conduct, it would be like trying to agree on how to put a swing set together in your backyard without a set of instructions. What a mess! However, Pam's husband claimed to have a set of instructions. He viewed himself as a follower of Jesus Christ and, as a result, was responsible to God's standard of behavior as it is found in the Bible. Therefore, Pam decided to challenge her husband on the basis of his marriage covenant with her and his expressed commitment to the Bible as his guide for life. The issue was not to be her viewpoint or my opinions. The issue was going to be God's Word over against his lifestyle.

The second thing we agreed must take place for reconciliation was Pam's husband's confession of wrongdoing and his sincere expression of his desire for Pam's forgiveness. This did not mean that Pam wanted to beat him over the head with his sin.

She was not going to demand that he come crawling back and tell her how much he had hurt her and their children. She did not feel it was her place to have him grovel and then to benevolently bestow forgiveness on him. Rather, we agreed that she needed to believe her husband was sincere. If he asked her to forgive him, he would have to mean it.

Can you understand Pam's need to feel her husband was sincere? If his confession wasn't genuine, any forgiveness that Pam might offer would be cheap forgiveness. Cheap forgiveness does not value a relationship. It wants only to alleviate pain. The motivation of such cheap forgiveness is to solve the pain of a broken relationship as soon as possible so that everyone might feel better.

Let me share a story of cheap forgiveness. It is about Frederick William, king of Prussia. Frederick was on his deathbed. A priest told him, "If you want to go to heaven, you must forgive your enemies."

When Frederick heard this, he immediately thought of his brother-in-law, George II of England. He hated his wife's brother. After giving the idea of forgiveness a few moments of thought, he turned to his wife and said, "I want you to write your brother. I want you to tell him that I forgive him. But please, do not write him until I am dead."

Cheap forgiveness: getting our problems solved as easily and conveniently as possible. Pam knew that this tactic would not heal the brokenness of her marriage. She needed to believe that her husband felt the same pain she felt over what he was doing to the family.

At the same time, Pam knew that she would have to request her husband's forgiveness. After all, she was not blameless in their problems. She needed to acknowledge where she had been wrong. She would have to show her husband that she was just as sincere in her confession of wrongdoing.

There was a third thing that Pam felt was necessary for the relationship with her husband to be reconciled. She felt they both needed to commit themselves to working on their relationship. Trust had to be rebuilt between them. After all, they had experienced a significant amount of hurt and pain over the past two years. It would take time before their faithfulness to each other would ratify the truth of their forgiveness. Time, hard work, and consistency of lifestyle could add up to a rebuilt trust and a strong marriage. Pam believed this was necessary if their reconciliation was to be genuine.

Let's review the three things that Pam felt were necessary for a real and honest reconciliation with her husband:

1. The honest acknowledgment by her husband that he had been violating his covenant commitment to her and the family, based on the Bible's standard of responsibility.

2. The need for him to confess his wrongdoing and sincerely express his desire for forgiveness.

3. The need for trust rebuilding in their relationship based on hard work, time invested in the marriage, and consistency of lifestyle over an extended period of time.

### My God, My Divorce, and Me

Perhaps you are wondering what all this talk on reconciliation has to do with God and your divorce. Well, earlier in this chapter, I commented that few people in the world are better prepared to understand the cost and difficulty involved in reconciliation than those who have been through a divorce. You can see this in Pam's story. And, after all, think of what it would take for you to be reconciled with your former spouse (if, indeed, a reconciliation could actually take place).

Now, did you know that God Himself has been through a divorce? Yes, that is true. I remember the first time I heard that startling fact. I was reading a book by Dr. Jay Adams entitled *Marriage, Divorce and Remarriage in the Bible*. In this book Dr. Adams makes the following statement:

> While God emphatically says, "I hate divorce" (Mal. 2:16), that statement must not be taken absolutely to mean that there is nothing about divorce that could be anything but detestable, because He, Himself, also tells us " . . . for all the adulteries which faithless Israel had done, I sent her away

and gave her a divorce bill" (Jer. 3:8, Berkeley). To
say, therefore, "I'll have nothing to do with divorced persons" is to speak irresponsibly and
places one in the nonissuable position of having
nothing to do with God, to boot! (He is a divorced
Person!) (pp. 23–24).

The problem in God's "marriage" with His people began with Adam and Eve. God had committed
Himself to our original parents in a covenant relationship not unlike a marriage covenant. Yet,
Adam and Eve rejected God. This, in and of itself,
was not a "divorce." But it was the first of a long
series of unfaithful actions by God's people. Ultimately, God had to officially divorce Himself from
the people to whom He had given His name! He
went through a divorce.

I hope that you grasp from this that God understands the pain and the difficulty of your divorce
more than you can imagine. He has also gone
through what you have experienced. Therefore,
God's response to you and your divorce is, first of
all, one of compassion and understanding.

However, we must not stop at this point of God's
understanding and experience of divorce. There
are deeper implications to God's divorce from His
people than the fact that He understands what you
have been through. For you see, the rejection of
God continues today. John 1:10–11 states, "He
[Jesus] was in the world, and the world was made
through Him, and the world did not know Him. He

came to His own, and His own did not receive Him."

Reflecting on the rejection of God by mankind, Paul wrote the following to the Romans: "[The people of the world] exchanged the truth of God for the lie, and worshiped and served the creature rather than the Creator, who is blessed forever" (1:25).

Now, as you read these verses you might be relieved by thinking, *Well, I have always tried to be good. I have always lived a relatively honest life (and after all, no one is perfect). I certainly haven't rejected God.*

My friend, starting with Adam and Eve, every human being who has ever lived fits into the verses quoted above! Every person who has been born on this earth (excluding Jesus Himself) has voted for independence from God rather than submit to His leadership. In essence, we treat God much like Pam's husband treated her. We want the marriage as long as we can have things our way.

Let me ask you one question. Would you like to be in a marriage like that? Would you like to be committed to someone who says that he will remain married to you as long as he can define the terms but he accepts no responsibility for the relationship? Of course not!

The poet John Keats once reflected on mankind's attitude toward God. Keats was on his deathbed. A friend asked him, "Do you believe God will forgive you?" The poet replied, "Of course

God will forgive me. Forgiveness is God's business."

In one sense, Keats was correct. God can and does forgive. But He doesn't offer cheap forgiveness. He doesn't say, "Go ahead. Live life any way you want to live without any thought of your responsibility to Me. I'll forgive you anyway."

No, God will not accept such a relationship with one of His creatures any more than you would accept such an arrangement for your marriage. Therefore, Paul noted in the book of Romans, "God gave them up to vile passions" (1:26). He was saying, "If you want a relationship with Me on the basis of your own standards and terms, then forget it! I am not interested!"

At the same time, the Bible extends to us the hope that we can have an honest and significant relationship with God. Earlier, I quoted John 1:10–11, which explains our rejection of God. However, the next verse from that passage reads as follows: "But as many as received Him, to them He gave the right to become children of God, to those who believe in His name" (v. 12).

## Belief in God

Belief in God incorporates the same three expectations that Pam felt were necessary to restore her marriage with her husband. First, it means we must honestly acknowledge that we are out of relationship with God. In the case of Pam's marriage, both husband and wife needed to recognize that there were real and significant problems in their relationship. Similarly, to believe in God, we must first recognize that there is a real problem in our relationship with God. We must acknowledge that we are alienated from God. The classic term for this alienation is *sin*.

The second part of belief is the need for the alienated parties to confess their wrongdoing and separation, and to seek forgiveness for the division in their relationship. In Pam's case, both parties needed to confess their wrongdoing. However, in our relationship with God the alienation comes from our side alone. God is not at fault here. As a matter of fact, God has gone out of His way to seek restoration even though mankind has rejected Him!

Have you ever realized that the reason Jesus Christ was born, lived, and died on the cross was to restore the relationship of God with man? Each of us has put God through the pain of a broken relationship. This pain is much deeper than what you or your former spouse might have inflicted on each other. God sent Jesus to earth to reestablish a relationship with us by extending the possibility of forgiveness and reconciliation. The cost to restore our relationship was not cheap. Jesus Christ died to take upon Himself the judgment of our alienation from God. In taking that judgment upon Himself, He provided the opportunity for our reconciliation.

When we realize what God went through to restore a relationship with each of us, and when we compare this with our own experience of alienation from our spouse (or former spouse), we should seriously ponder our response. We must not look upon such a sacrifice in a light or superficial way. We should openly confess that our relationship with Him has been broken. We should ask Him for forgiveness and for the reconciliation necessary for an honest and open relationship. We can ask for this only on the basis of the sacrifice He has made to bring this reconciliation about.

The third element in belief is trust rebuilding. Pam and her husband would have to work together to reestablish trust in their marriage. In the same way, after we acknowledge our alienation from God and then seek God's forgiveness, we need to work at strengthening our relationship with God. This can be done by spending time in prayer and meditating on the Bible. Prayer and Bible meditation are equivalent to the time a husband and wife spend in communication. In prayer we have the opportunity to share heart concerns with God. The Bible is full of encouragement for men and women to pray in this manner. For example, the psalmist says,

Give ear to my words, O LORD,

Consider my meditation.
Give heed to the voice of my cry,
My King and my God,
For to You I will pray.
My voice You shall hear in the
   morning, O LORD;
In the morning I will direct it to You,
And I will look up (Ps. 5:1–3).

Similarly, Paul motivates the Philippians to pray by declaring, "Be anxious for nothing, but in everything by prayer and supplication, with thanksgiving, let your requests be made known to God; and the peace of God, which surpasses all understanding, will guard your hearts and minds through Christ Jesus" (Phil. 4:6–7).

Through meditation on the Bible, we learn of God's heart concerns for us. The psalmist expressed the importance of such meditation when he said, "The entrance of Your words gives light; it gives understanding to the simple" (Ps. 119:130).

When reconciliation takes place between two people, the result is a sense of warmth and unity that was missing before they had a problem in their relationship. If you believe in God by acknowledging your separation from Him, by confessing this separation and seeking His forgiveness, and by maintaining a relationship with Him, you are going to experience a special type of joy that transcends circumstances.

Even in the midst of the deep pain of divorce this relationship with God can be to you like a spring of refreshing water within your very being. I do not mean you will have a ridiculous grin on your face all of the time. Nor do I mean you will feel wonderful all the time. What I mean is that the compass of your soul will be set on a direct course with the Lord of the universe. You will be in a right relationship with God.

What will such a relationship mean as you experience the slippery slope on your way toward acceptance? It means that God will provide you with at least three things: forgiveness, acceptance, and strength.

### Knowing You Are Forgiven

We live in a society under the constant strain of guilt. And you know the guilt that you can experience in a divorce: guilt over past failures and present mistakes. However, God has promised a continual flow of forgiveness and restoration from guilt as you seek to please Him.

One verse I turn to regularly is 1 John 1:9. I memorized this verse a number of years ago, and I encourage you to do the same thing. Listen to this tremendous promise: "If we confess our sins, He is faithful and just to forgive us our sins and to cleanse us from all unrighteousness."

This promise says that we do not have to live under a continual weight of guilt. Of course, it does not absolve us from our responsibility to resolve conflict and wrongdoing. But it does promise that there is nothing we can do that will not be forgiven.

We must not forget about cheap forgiveness, though. The promise of God's forgiveness must not be taken as license to do whatever we please. However, God has committed Himself to respond to our confession and cleanse us from all that we have done wrong. What a fantastic resource He provides!

### Acceptance

I have often had friends share this thought with me: "I can't understand how God can accept and love me after all I have done."

There must have been times when the apostle Paul had the same feelings. At one point he even told his friend Timothy that he was the chief of sinners. That meant Paul felt he was the most notorious sinner who ever lived. Yet, at the same time Paul knew that God did accept him. Listen to his words:

> This is a faithful saying and worthy of all acceptance, that Christ Jesus came into the world to save sinners, of whom I am chief. However, for this reason I obtained mercy, that in me first Jesus Christ might show all longsuffering, as a pattern to those who are going to believe on Him for everlasting life (1 Tim. 1:15–16).

Paul says to each of us, "Do you have a hard time believing that God would accept you? Well, He accepted me, and I serve as an example to you. If He could accept me, He will accept you as well."

A friend shared an illustration that helped me understand God's acceptance. He said, "You are the son of your parents. Regardless of what you might ever do, nothing can erase the fact that you are the son of your father and mother. They will always be your parents. In the same way, God, through Christ, calls us His children. He claims to be our Father. Once you are in the family of God, nothing can take you out of the family. Jesus said, 'I am the good shepherd; and I know My sheep, and am known by My own. . . . And I give them eternal life, and they shall never perish; neither shall anyone snatch them out of My hand' (John 10:14, 28)."

This is acceptance. If you have gone through separation and divorce, you know what rejection means. If you are in the family of God, you can know what acceptance means.

## Strength

I know few people who need strength more than those who are going through the whirlwind of separation and divorce. You need strength to handle emotional difficulties, strength to face the future, strength to parent children whose family life has been shattered. The list of needs for strength could go on and on.

I find it interesting to read in the Bible how often people have been in circumstances where they had to cry out for strength. One example is found in 2 Corinthians. Paul, the apostle, is the author. He shared with his friends in Corinth the challenges that he and his associates had been facing: "For we do not want you to be ignorant, brethren, of our trouble which came to us in Asia: that we were burdened beyond measure, above strength, so that we despaired even of life. Yes, we had the sentence of death in ourselves" (2 Cor. 1:8–9a).

I am sure that you relate to Paul's concerns in these verses! You know what it means to be under great pressure, beyond your ability to endure. You probably have even despaired of life. Well, you are in good company with Paul and his associates. Now, listen to what Paul wrote next: "That we should not trust in ourselves but in God who raises the dead" (v. 9b).

Paul said that the very circumstances causing him to despair of life itself had been designed by God to force him to look beyond himself. Think of it! It is possible that the problems you have faced over the past weeks (or even months) have been divinely prepared to teach you how to look to God for help.

Furthermore, Paul explains that God is One we can confidently rely upon for strength. After all, God can raise the dead! What higher level of power is needed? And He who raises the dead is ready to help us in our time of need.

Now, you might be thinking, *God is too busy to concern Himself with my little world. Of course He was there for Paul. Paul was important. But why should He be there for me?*

He is there for you! You mean so much to Him that He sent Jesus to die so that you might be reconciled to Him (John 3:16). And He is there for you because He promised to show you this kind of concern (Rom. 8:20; Phil. 1:6). In the Sermon on the Mount, Jesus said, "Look at the birds of the air, for they neither sow nor reap nor gather into barns; yet your heavenly Father feeds them. Are you not of more value than they?" (Matt. 6:26).

Because you are significant to God, He plans to provide you with the strength necessary to do His will. There is a special promise that God has given to all of His people recorded in Isaiah 41:10. Listen to it and apply it to yourself. God says,

> Fear not, for I am with you;
> Be not dismayed, for I am your God.
> I will strengthen you,
> Yes, I will help you,
> I will uphold you with My righteous
>     right hand.

This is a promise for anyone who is a child of God. It is particularly relevant for those who are going through the whirlwind of a crisis experience. The apostle Paul had to lean hard on God while going through the whirlwind. We must learn this as well so that we may say together with Paul, "I can do all things through Christ who strengthens me" (Phil. 4:13).

### Playing Christian Versus Knowing God

We have been reviewing the resources available to those who have a restored relationship with God. However, in order to tap these resources we must examine ourselves to know whether we are truly children of God or simply religious persons.

Once I heard a story about Leonardo da Vinci that helped me understand this difference between knowing God and being religious. One of da Vinci's beloved paintings is of the Last Supper. It portrays the time when Jesus Christ ate His final meal with His disciples. And to make the painting as lifelike as possible, he chose various models to pose as Christ and His disciples.

The first figure da Vinci decided to paint was Jesus Christ. To find the right model he interviewed hundreds of people. The face of this man had to represent purity, contentment, gentleness, compassion, and mercy. He finally found one man whom he felt would properly depict Jesus. Over a period of six months, the master carefully painted each detail of the Christ-figure.

Then da Vinci went on to paint each of the disciples. For seven years he labored to reproduce the scene. Finally, he came to the last figure to paint: Judas, the traitor of Jesus.

Again da Vinci faced a problem. He had to find someone who was so twisted and distorted in mind and body that he would model the agony, pain, and torture of Judas when he decided to betray Christ. Again Leonardo searched and searched, but he could not find the right man. Then one day he heard of a criminal in jail for multiple murders. The man was scheduled for execution in Rome.

Da Vinci went to the prison in Rome. When he saw the man, he was convinced that this was the only person who could represent Judas. So he went to the king and received a temporary pardon from execution long enough to complete the painting.

Day after day the man, chained to his guards, was brought to da Vinci. He was not allowed to speak. He could only sit for the painting. However, da Vinci was only able to paint for a few hours each day. The man would often start screaming and yanking on his chains. The guards would have to drag him back to the prison.

After long months of work, the painting of Judas was complete. The guards were preparing to take the prisoner back to his cell for the final time. He was to be executed the next day. Just as he was about to be taken from the room, the man broke loose. He ran up to the great artist and fell at his feet, clutching his legs. The prisoner cried out, "Leonardo, don't you know who I am?" Da Vinci replied, "Sir, I have never seen you before the day I came into the prison and chose you to model."

The man moaned, "Have I fallen so far?" Then he looked back up at the artist and said, "You don't recognize me? I am the man who sat for you seven years ago while you were painting the face of Jesus Christ!"

In a graphic way this story illustrates that it is possible to pose as a Christian but never really have a relationship with God. Like the model, someone can look very righteous. But the difference is found in the heart. Sooner or later the condition of his heart will catch up with him, and his lifestyle will reflect that condition.

## An Opportunity for Growth

The purpose of this book has been to help you better understand what you have been through so that you might use the difficulties and struggles of separation and divorce for your personal growth. It has also been my hope that you could learn more of the God who loves you. He wants to demonstrate His love in providing the forgiveness, acceptance, and strength necessary for you to make the most out of a difficult life experience. Dr. Paul Tournier summarizes this opportunity in his book *Creative Suffering:* "It is in coming to Jesus that each of us finds the courage to recognize ourselves for what we are, and then to accept ourselves because we are accepted, pardoned and loved by Jesus just as we are" (p. 107).

A few years ago Gloria Gaither penned a beautiful verse that expresses the difference a restored relationship with God can have for personal recovery and growth. She wrote,

> I am loved, I am loved,
>   I can risk loving you.
> For the One who knows me best
>   loves me most.

Coming into a relationship with the living God is not a quick fix. It is not another bargain where you find an easy solution to a complex problem. All of life's hassles will still be there as real as ever before. The difference comes from within. You become a person in whom God Himself is at work. As you become more like Him, you grow into more wholeness. This process will not be finished until the time when God brings all things into completion (Rom. 8:23). However, prior to this time of perfection, we can sing out with an elderly black man, once a slave, who was heard praying:

> Oh God, I ain't what I should be;
> And God, I ain't what I could be;
> But God, thanks that I ain't what I used to be!

# APPENDIX A

# A Biblical Mandate for Ministry to the Separated and Divorced

Noah was loading the animals into his ark, on board they went two by two. Imagine how it might have felt being an unpaired animal in line. There you would have been, alone and rejected, while the other animals entered the craft. You would have been left off the ark.

The Christian who is single again through divorce often feels left off the ark of God's church. In the church, marriage is the socially acceptable status, even if the marriage is in shambles. When the single who has been married enters the church, he or she often feels like the odd one out.

When the Bible addresses the issue of divorce, it approaches the topic from two mutually dependent perspectives. The first perspective is that of doctrine. This is extremely important, for doctrine must always form one's foundation for living.

In our day it is crucial for the church to grapple with her theological convictions regarding divorce. The believer in the pew is looking for clear

159

understanding and direction in this matter. With a national average of close to 50 percent of all marriages failing in 1987, each denomination and each local congregation must clearly explain its position on this nationwide epidemic. Such a clarification before God's people will solidify their conviction before a personal, congregational, or denominational crisis occurs. It will also fortify their ability to deal with problems when they take place.

At the same time another biblical perspective coordinates with the doctrinal imperative. It is the relational side of divorce. By highlighting the relational concerns of divorce, I do not wish to create an implied barrier between doctrine and life. But it is far too easy to examine the theology of divorce while remaining isolated from persons involved in it. This, too, can create an artificial separation of doctrine and life.

The relational concerns of divorce do not simply refer to the way a couple handle their differences. They also refer to the way believers in Christ are called by the Scriptures to care for those who are going through or have gone through the wrenching death of a relationship.

The prophet Malachi says that God hates divorce (Mal. 2:16). But does God call His people to treat those shattered by such a covenant breaking with the same hatred? It is my thesis that both Old and New Testaments mandate God's people to give themselves in compassionate ministry to the separated and divorced. Because of this mandate, the church must take specific restorative action to maintain corporate health and an effective witness in the world.

## The Old Testament Mandate

In the Old Testament divorce is neither encouraged nor condoned. Rather, it is viewed as the shattering of a commitment that was meant to be forever.

It was not a simple matter. The impact it would have upon the individuals involved and the community as a whole was taken quite seriously. A number of passages, including Genesis 3, Leviticus 18, Deuteronomy 24, Jeremiah 3, and Malachi 2, are normally cited with reference to the Old Testament perspective on divorce. Indeed, these texts must be considered in formulating a doctrinal position on marital separation. They state the moral context of divorce, describing it as the breaking of a marriage covenant, and also provide the legal context of divorce, with the steps of litigation necessary for proper regulation and protection of each party described in detail.

However, these passages cited above do not provide us with the full understanding of the care and concern that God required His people to give to those who were being divorced. Such a perspective can be clarified when we study the contextual use of the Hebrew word for widow, *almanah*. This word refers to a woman who has been divested of her male protector, usually though not always through death. But the *Assyrian Dictionary of The University of Chicago Oriental Institute* states that *almanah* does not simply refer to a woman whose husband is dead. It also applies to a woman who enjoys no financial support from a male member of her family. Such a woman is in need of legal protection. She is also able to exercise freedom by starting a profession or entering into a second marriage. Thus, the word can be used in the sense of bereavement (such as loss of a spouse) or for one who has been discarded or forsaken (such as a divorced person).

This interpretation of *almanah* as the widowed or abandoned fits several Old Testament passages. For example, when God forsook His people and their land, they were characterized as *almanah*, "widow" (Isa. 47:8), and their situation as *almanuth* (Isa. 54:4). But Israel's "husband" had not passed away! Rather, He had written her a certificate of divorce (Jer. 3:8). Similarly, when King David returned to Jerusalem after Absalom's revolt, "the king took the ten women [with whom Absalom had committed adultery] . . . and put them in seclusion and supported them, but did not go in to them. So they were shut up to the day of their death, *living in widowhood* (2 Sam. 20:3, italics added). Technically, these then were in widowhood while their husbands were still alive. All of this is to say the Old Testament taught that the forsaken spouse was considered in the same category as the widow.

The implications of this connection between the forsaken and the widow are powerful indeed because the Old Testament is full of God's concerns and commands for the widow. God declared that He would execute justice for the widow (Deut. 10:18; Prov. 15:25), and He required His people to do so, also (Isa. 1:17; Jer. 7:5–6; 22:3; Zech. 7:10). He would punish those who refused to do so (Isa. 1:23–25; Mal. 3:5). His people were to provide for the physical needs of the widow (Deut. 14:28–29; 24:19–22). God was clearly on the side of the widow (Pss. 68:5; 146:9), and He expected His people to be as well.

The Old Testament also addressed the member of the marriage covenant who was initiating the abandonment. While it described the proper legal procedure these individuals were to take in order to obtain a divorce, it also provided for legal discipline within the community directed toward those who had abandoned their covenant responsibility to their spouse.

It is beyond the scope of this Appendix to explicate the detailed instructions in the Law given for specific offenses. It must suffice to say that God took a firm stand for justice toward the oppressed, and God expected His people to administer justice in a meaningful way. With regard to divorce, others have shown that legal stipulations encouraged a lengthy and systematic procedure that sought to ensure both justice for the forsaken spouse and public responsibility for the one taking action.

## The New Testament Mandate

The New Testament carried on the tradition of the Old regarding the treatment of divorced persons. But it went further, clarifying how God's people were to deal with all parties in the divorce.

First, let's consider Jesus' attitude toward the divorced as seen in the story of the woman at the well (John 4). Here we observe our Lord initiating a conversation with a woman who had been married five times and was currently living in an adulterous relationship with yet another man.

We find a balance in Jesus' ministry with this woman. On the one hand, we notice that He understood her circumstances and feelings. He knew of her previous marriages and her present adultery. But He did not use these against her. Rather, Jesus' honest and open handling of her situation broke through her emotional and religious smoke screens of resistance, preparing her to hear the word of truth.

Furthermore Jesus demonstrated an honest concern for this woman by breaking significant cultural taboos in order to communicate with her. He spoke in the open with a woman whose husband was not present (a questionable act in the Middle East to this day). She was also a "despised Samaritan." And to make matters worse, she was a flagrant sinner! But Jesus did not allow these social matters to keep Him from sharing with her the good news.

On the other hand, Jesus never condoned the woman's sin. He initiated the topic of her loose morality. Perhaps He delved into more of her past than we read in the narrative, for she later reported, "He told me everything I ever did." Our Lord refused to carry on a superficial conversation when both He and the woman knew of her circumstances.

According to John 1:14, Jesus ministered with grace and truth. Revealing His understanding of the woman's condition, He spoke with candor and truth. Yet truth was couched in the grace of His power to cleanse and restore wholeness. This combination of caring acceptance and honest confrontation prepared her for the life change of conversion.

The response of this woman is phenomenal. She confessed her sin by returning to the town and owning up to her past. In addition, she urged everyone to come and see this Man. It is obvious that significant healing had taken place in her life. Past failure and weakness provided the bases of ministry to others.

We must acknowledge that this entire scene took place because our Savior extended Himself to

one who had been divorced. He initiated the conversation. He disclosed the truth of her circumstances. He led her to an understanding of life
fulfillment beyond the disappointment of a broken
marriage or a new sexual liaison.

Following our Lord's example, a similar pattern
of ministry to the rejected took place in the early
church. In 1 Corinthians 6, Paul explained that
some of the new believers had come out of a vari-
ety of backgrounds including sexual immorality,
adultery, thievery and other sordid lifestyles. (He
did not include divorce in this list, but his obvious
concern with their circumstances in the next chapter must mean that many in this situation were
within the fellowship.) Like the woman at the well,
these people who knew they were sinners grasped
for the gospel of grace with eagerness.

An examination of other New Testament writers
highlights the same theme: spiritual rebirth extends hope to the rejected, healing to the broken-
hearted, and opportunities for meaningful service
to those who once thought their lives had little significance.

While the New Testament described the gospel
as a source of renewal, it also provided for a specific framework for parties involved in divorce. It
addressed the problem of mixed marriages between believer and nonbeliever (1 Cor. 7). It expli-
cated the restorative role that church discipline
should take in the life of God's people (Matt.
18:15–20; 1 Cor. 5:1–5; 2 Cor. 2:5–11). It required

the appointment of church leaders who were expected to provide a supportive context where difficult issues would be handled before God with objectivity and compassion (Matt. 18:15–20; Acts 20:28; 1 Cor. 6:1–6; Heb. 13:17; 1 Pet. 5:2–4).

We have observed that the New Testament developed the expectation of the Old. God's people were to extend themselves to those in the agony of divorce. Although the church was never to tolerate sin, she was to provide a context where the conditions preceding (and following) divorce would be handled. At the same time she was responsible to follow the lead of the Lord Jesus, who actively sought out and ministered to divorced persons.

## The Mandate in Our Day

Both Old and New Testaments affirm the church's need to actively involve herself in the divorce recovery process. To fulfill this role, the church must evaluate and implement change in three areas: her attitudes, her discipline, and her program ministries.

The last ten years have marked significant attitudinal changes in the church. Some believers have developed a tolerance of divorce for any reason. This "do your own thing" mentality does not square with faithfulness to Christ's lordship. Such "liberation" is not the attitudinal change needed among believers today. Neither is there a need for hardened insensitivity that writes off all persons going through divorce as sinners who no longer hold an equal position in the church.

Rather, the mind-set necessary toward the divorced individual is one of practical grace. Practical grace is the humility of recognizing that every believer stands before God in need of mercy. No one person is better than another at the foot of the cross.

While most Christians would affirm this concept of grace in theory, the practical side means applying the truth of Godward acceptance toward our relationships with others. Developing an attitude of practical grace means we must beware lest we take on the attitude of the boasting Pharisee in Luke 18:10–14 who said, "God, I thank You that I am not like other men." It also requires that we treat the divorced person in the same way Jesus Christ has treated us: redeeming us from our past failures, forgiving us for our present sin, and challenging us to live and relate on the basis of the truth revealed in His Word.

Acceptance can never be based on anything less than our mutual submission to Jesus Christ. When this is the standard, a caring attitude toward the divorced should follow. Where divorced persons experience rejection simply on the basis of their single-again status, a church should examine herself as to her understanding of justification in practical terms.

A partner of attitudinal change must be restorative discipline. Restorative discipline is the church's corporate responsibility to maintain the standard of God's Word as her lifestyle pattern. It is unfortunate that God's people tend to view discipline as either a method of punishment or a theoretical idea rarely put into practice. The scriptural imperative for church discipline is restoration: to bring a fallen member back to the full status of an active participant in the fellowship. Only with this restorative purpose in view can discipline be used as an effective tool in the reconciliation of marriages and in the care of those shattered by divorce.

Restorative discipline takes hard work. It is one of the most taxing responsibilities of the church. The process is outlined in Matthew 18:15–20. It begins with reconciliation on a one-to-one basis. If this attempt fails, one or two believers are to be called on as objective arbitrators. If that is unsuccessful, the final step is to bring the matter before the church (which requires the involvement of the church leadership).

This process demands cooperation from the entire body of believers. When a member seeks the aid of a fellow believer to intercede in a divided relationship, the one requested must be willing to participate. It is one thing to express concern. It is quite another to diminish one's personal comfort through involvement with another!

If the situation continues to deteriorate, the church leaders must take action. This will demand extended time and effort if they are to properly understand, negotiate, and exercise authority. Such an oversight role is often much more than a typical board member expected when he agreed to serve. Yet this is vital care for those who turn to their church for help in a crisis.

If the problem comes before the entire congregation, there is a need for each member to clearly understand and consistently follow through on the decision of the fellowship. And of course, with all of these dynamics there is the added requirement of keeping restoration, not vindication, as the purpose of the procedure.

If discipline is so difficult, why is it necessary? First of all, it is necessary because it is God's provision for maintaining a healthy lifestyle in the church. If the body of believers is to take seriously its faithfulness to God's Word, it must deal biblically with circumstances that flagrantly violate scriptural responsibilities. Without this, all admonitions to faithfulness take the form of empty words with no moral authority to substantiate the exhortation.

A second reason for discipline is to provide a supportive context for the ones involved in the marital dissension. Where will the battered wife turn when she desires to remain faithful yet fears for her life? Where will the believing husband receive counsel when he is struggling with a decision to contest his divorce? Where will the separated Christian turn when faced with the desire to date after the failure of his marriage seems a foregone conclusion? Conscientious Christians in these types of circumstances welcome the network of support and counsel offered by God's people when it is available. The painful fact, however, is that thousands of Christians who honestly desire such objective guidance and encouragement from the church receive the answer that other believers don't want to get involved.

In separation and divorce there is rarely, if ever a case where one party is beyond reproach and the other should receive total blame for the failure. Marriage is a shared responsibility, and those involved in church discipline must labor to maintain joint accountability as the issues are handled. At the same time, in most divorce cases only one partner seeks the aid of the church. For this person the discipline should not create deeper guilt but should provide a healthy context for restoration so that the person can maintain the status of a fully functioning member of Christ's church in the process.

In the meantime, what is the purpose of discipline toward the one who lacks any desire for the church's involvement? It is to win the brother or sister back through a prolonged concerned call for accountability to the lifestyle promises he or she acknowledged in church membership and in marital vows.

Jesus declared that He came to give abundant life. He expected His people to be part of this life-giving and life-restoring process. Restorative discipline means the use of the authority of the church for the purpose of bringing persons back to such a state of wholeness. It is difficult. It is exhausting. It demands a long-term commitment. But it is an imperative if the church is to fulfill her ministry to the divorced.

A third change point for the church to explore is in the area of program ministries. Distinct from the need for attitudinal change and restorative discipline, program ministries deal with the ongoing expression of the church in the form of her activities and schedule.

What is happening in the church on a regular basis for the divorced and separated in the congregation? Planned activities can communicate to these people that the congregation cares for them and is ready to invest the effort necessary to meet their needs. Such programs validate the full role that the congregation feels these persons have in the fellowship. Weekly Bible studies, single-parent support groups, classes for singles in the Sunday school curriculum, and divorce recovery seminars are examples of some useful programs. Some churches with multistaff capabilities are beginning to hire full-time professionals to serve in the area of single adult ministries.

The church must also assume responsibilities to establish programs of outreach to the separated and divorced of the community. It has been observed that the divorce experience is a complex process during which further personality growth can take place. Old lifestyle patterns and goals that were once assumed are challenged during this time of transition. Such reevaluation provides an exceptional context for thoughtful consideration of the gospel if the church is prepared to contact such persons at their point of need. Creative programs must be explored on this point.

The form that any particular church would decide to use in a ministry to single-again persons is not at issue here. Rather, the concern is for the divorced and separated persons in the congregation and the surrounding community to sense that a redemptive fellowship is prepared to take action on their behalf. When this concern is present and expressed, the details of specific programs will work out themselves according to the various situations.

# APPENDIX B

# The Validity of Using the Stages of Grief Model

After the presentation of the *slippery slope* in a Fresh Start Seminar, occasionally some people are concerned about my use of the five-stage model of emotional recovery. Their concern generally focuses on two issues.

The first is that the model is based on modern-day psychology and not on the Bible. This concern is valid since the Bible is the Christian's standard of authority. Any viewpoint contrary to the Bible cannot be considered Christian.

I believe that the use of the stages of grief model is justified as long as it accurately reflects true experience and God-given emotional responses while not directly or indirectly contradicting Scripture. Actually, I have used the model because I see it implicitly reflected throughout the Bible. Granted, it is not directly presented in any single chapter or verse. However, neither are many doctrines studied in systematic theology! Rather, these doctrines are deduced from numerous passages as clear principles and implications. For example, the doctrine of the Trinity is not directly presented in any particular passage, but a thorough study of Scripture will lead to the obvious conclusion of the Bible's trinitarian thrust.

In a similar (though much less profound) way the model can be deduced from Scripture. For example, Peter struggled with denial when he said, "Far be it from You, Lord; this shall not happen to You!" in response to Jesus' teaching on His suffering and death (Matt. 16:22). And Elijah battled with depression after his defeat of the prophets of Baal on Mount Carmel (1 Kings 18). I suggest that the model is not superimposing secular psychology on the biblical data. It simply codifies the natural emotional responses of people in a somewhat systematic order for understanding and clarity.

The second issue focuses on the best-known presentation of the stages of grief model by Dr. Elisabeth Kübler-Ross. Many of Dr. Kübler-Ross's books written since the publication of *On Death and Dying* (where she presents the five-stage model) have material in variance with the Scriptures. Some individuals state that it is dangerous to use a model prepared by a person espousing nonbiblical viewpoints.

My response is to appreciate the primary concern that the Bible's authority not be watered down by a "secularist" perspective. I applaud this concern, but I do not think it should prevent our use of the model.

The concept of emotional grieving stages did not originate with Dr. Kübler-Ross. Although she popularized the theory in her book, the idea of grief stages was first suggested in 1940 by Dr. Erich Lindeman of Harvard University. Many researchers have found common coping patterns among persons in life crises. And as I mentioned in chapter 4, there are no less than twelve different theories suggested by as many authors with reference to divorce. These theories vary in emphasis and complexity, but their essential differences are minor.

Therefore, the issue is not with Dr. Kübler-Ross. She simply appropriated accepted research with her own observations and reported them in a way that the public could understand. As I previously said, the real issue is whether or not the model adequately reflects true experience and God-given emotional responses without directly or indirectly contradicting Scripture. I believe the stages of grief model properly fulfills these criteria. So I feel confident it can be used in a manner that pleases God and enhances the truth of the Bible.

# REFERENCES

Adams, Jay E. *Marriage, Divorce and Remarriage in the Bible*. Grand Rapids, Mich.: Zondervan, 1980, pp. 27–31.

Bowlby, John. "Affectional Bonds: Their Nature and Origin" in *Loneliness*, ed. Robert W. Weiss. Cambridge: MIT Press, 1973, p. 40.

Collins, Gary R. *Christian Counseling: A Comprehensive Guide*. Waco, Tex.: Word, 1980, p. 104.

Dastell, Joan C. "Stress Reactions to Marital Dissolution as Experienced by Adults Attending Courses on Divorce" in *Journal of Divorce*, vol. 5, no. 3 (Spring 1982), p. 46.

Fisher, Bruce. *Rebuilding*. San Luis Obispo: Impact Publishers, 1981.

Frederico, Joseph. "The Marital Termination Period of the Divorce Adjustment Process" in *Journal of Divorce*, vol. 3, no. 2 (Winter 1979), p. 103.

Gangsei, Lyle B. *Manual for Group Pre-Marital Counsel-*

*ing.* New York: Association Press, 1971. Quoted by
H. Norman Wright in *Pre-Marital Counseling.* Chicago:
Moody Press, 1977, p. 179.

Gelb, Ignance J., ed. "almattu" in *Assyrian Dictionary of
the University of Chicago Oriental Institute*, vol. 1, part 1.
Chicago: The Oriental Institute of the University of Chicago, 1964, pp. 362–364.

Gray, Gloria. "The Nature of the Psychological Impact
of Divorce Upon the Individual." *Journal of Divorce*, vol.
1, no. 4 (Summer 1978), p. 299.

Hoffner, Harry A. "almana" in *Theological Dictionary of
the Old Testament*, rev. ed., vol. 1. G. Johannes Bot-
tenweck and Helmen Ringgren, eds., John T. Wills,
trans. Grand Rapids, Mich.: Eerdmans, 1977, pp.
287–291.

Tournier, Paul. *The Meaning of Persons.* New York:
Harper and Row, 1957, p. 55.

Strong, James. *Exhaustive Concordance of the Bible, Hebrew and Chaldee Dictionary.* Marchallton: The National Foundation for Christian Education, n.d.

Wallerstein, Judith S., and Sandra Blakeslee. *Second
Chances.* New York: Ticknor and Fields, 1989, p. xii.

Walters, Richard P. *Anger: Yours and Mine and What to
Do About It.* Grand Rapids, Mich.: Zondervan, 1981.

# STUDY GUIDE

## Preface

**P. 1**  Write a few sentences explaining why you are interested in reading this book.

**P. 2**  In the Preface the author comments that many of us feel we deserve to be happy, yet we know it is unrealistic to avoid problems in life (p. viii). In other words, we think we should be happy, yet we know we cannot always be happy.

Do you experience this ambivalence? Why? How has your separation or divorce intensified it?

## Introduction

I.1   The author compares divorce with the
      story of Dorothy in *The Wizard of Oz*. Life
      was normal before the whirlwind. Now
      things are strange, new, and different
      (p. xii).

      Take a piece of paper and draw a line
      down the center. On the top left side write
      *Before* and on the top right put *After*. Jot
      down words or phrases describing life be-
      fore and after your divorce.

      Keep this list handy as you read the book.
      Add to it as you would like.

I.2   The author states that his purpose is to
      help make your divorce an occasion for
      growth rather than crippling (p. xiii).

      So far, do you feel crippled by your di-
      vorce, or do you feel you are growing
      through it? Why?

## Chapter One: What Am I Going Through?

1.1     Peter said, "Everything I counted on was lost" (p. 15). Even though it is painful, it is good to recount your losses experienced in divorce.

On the "Before and After" page you started, jot down things you have lost (or gained) by your divorce. Some of these might be: a job, friends, status, financial security, children.

1.2     When have you felt powerless? What were the reasons?

1.3     Here the author describes a crisis as a time when the steady state of life is disrupted (p. 16). How does your "Before and After" page affirm this definition?

At this point you might feel that your life before separation was very steady. How negative or positive was your steady state before separation? Why?

**1.4**   At the bottom of page 17 the author states that a crisis experience will always change you. Review the "Before and After" page you started, adding ways your life has been changed by your divorce.

Review the changes you have written down, putting a + next to the changes you view as positive and a − next to the ones you view as negative.

**1.5**   Marital separation is different from the death of a spouse. Closure is more difficult. Divorce is not socially acceptable. It creates an open wound (p. 19).

What are some of the open wounds you still feel from the breakup of your marriage?

**1.6**   Divorce is a crisis experience (p. 19). Many going through it have experienced the efforts of well-meaning friends or acquaintances to minimize divorce by making remarks like: "Oh, come on, get over it" or "Stop feeling so sad; life goes on."

How have you experienced this minimizing of divorce?

1.7    Peter's parents didn't handle his divorce
       very well. They took his divorce as their
       personal failure (p. 20).

       How has your family responded to your
       divorce? List specific names of family
       members and their responses to you.

1.8    On a scale of one to ten rate yourself on
       how well you feel you have coped with
       your marital breakup.

          1 = I have done a great job! No hassles,
              bitterness, or anger.
         10 = I have really blown it. It seems that
              everything I do is a mistake. I feel
              betrayed by and angry at everything
              and everybody, including myself.

       If you have a friend or a family member
       who has been close to you through your
       marital separation, ask this person to rate
       you on this coping scale. Then talk to-
       gether about your perceptions of how you
       have handled things.

1.10   What persons have you found most sup-
       portive and encouraging through your di-
       vorce?

What persons have hurt or disappointed you in the midst of your divorce?

1.11    Consider the following quotation: "Personal maturity is, in a large measure, the result of successful crisis resolutions" (p. 23).

Write reasons you agree or disagree with this statement.

1.12    Growth requires honesty about how you feel and what you believe. Record your honest thoughts and feelings as you read the following statement: "When one knows that God is in control, crisis can become a divinely designed opportunity" (p. 25).

## Chapter Two: The Mating Game

2.1     How would you define *love?*

Suppose a friend came to you considering marriage for the first time and said, "I think I love him, but I'm not sure." How would you respond?

According to your definition of *love*, would you say you were in love when you got married? Why? Why not?

2.2   What do the statistics on divorce in our society (p. 28) tell us about our understanding of love?

2.3   Respond to the following statement: "Most people . . . marry for romantic-passionate reasons" (p. 28).

From the perspective of your experience, what are some things besides romance that people ought to consider before marriage?

2.4   How should marriage at least partially

fulfill our God-given need for relationship
(p. 29)?

2.5    Since your separation/divorce, how have
       you handled feelings of loneliness?


       Who are your three best friends?


2.6    As you look back on it now, how well did
       you know your fiancé and his or her fam-
       ily prior to engagement?


2.7    What was engagement like for you? What
       occupied your time and thoughts?


       How well prepared were you for mar-
       riage?


2.8    If you could turn back the clock, what
       changes would you make in your time of

dating and engagement? What would you
do differently? What questions would you
ask? What would you want to learn more
about?

2.9     Do you feel you took the wedding vows se-
        riously, or were they simply a ritual in the
        wedding service? Why?

2.10    The bonds between marriage partners
        can become very strong (p. 34). Do you
        have a continued sense of bondedness to
        your former spouse? If you don't feel this
        now, have you experienced it in the past?

## Chapter Three: Till Death Do Us Part
### (The Decision to Divorce)

3.1     Before your separation or divorce what
        were some of the pat answers you would
        give about the marital problems of
        others?

**3.2**  What are three or four ways you have become aware of issues and difficulties in
others' lives as a result of your divorce?




**3.3**  Five common reasons are given for seeking divorce (pp. 39–44). Rate these five on
the following scale. Then try to add at
least two other reasons specific to your
situation.

1 = Not important in my divorce
3 = Played a part in my divorce
5 = Significant reason for my divorce

| | | | | | |
|---|---|---|---|---|---|
| 1. No longer friends | 1 | 2 | 3 | 4 | 5 |
| 2. Decreased trust | 1 | 2 | 3 | 4 | 5 |
| 3. Poor communication | 1 | 2 | 3 | 4 | 5 |
| 4. Lack of shared goals | 1 | 2 | 3 | 4 | 5 |
| 5. Discontinued marital intimacy | 1 | 2 | 3 | 4 | 5 |
| Other reasons: | | | | | |
| 6. | 1 | 2 | 3 | 4 | 5 |
| 7. | 1 | 2 | 3 | 4 | 5 |

**3.4**  Many separated and divorced persons ask
themselves: *Have I given or did I give reconciliation my best shot? Could I or
should I have done anything else to keep
my marriage together?*

On pages 44–46 six necessary areas of cooperation for marital health are presented. Both parties in a marriage must be involved in these six areas for reconciliation. Review these areas and evaluate how much you and your (former) spouse have been willing to work on them. Give each category a high, medium, or low rating.

High      Willing to do whatever it takes to make it happen
Medium    Willing to work on it but exhibits some resistance
Low       Resistant or unwilling to work on this area

If you have a hard time rating an area, think of its opposite characteristic. For example, the opposite of honesty is dishonesty: the refusal to acknowledge personal problems and differences.

| Area of Cooperation | Your Involvement | Your Spouse's Involvement |
| --- | --- | --- |
| Honesty—admitting problems and differences | | |
| Negotiation of differences—open dialogue about | | |

differences rather
than hardened
demands

Accepting the
unchangeable in
the other

Giving in—
overlooking
personal rights for
the sake of the
relationship

Investment of time
and energy in doing
these things

Repentance—
recognizing and
acknowledging
mistakes, with a
commitment to
change

3.5    Would you call yourself the active agent
       or the passive agent in your divorce
       (pp. 49–50)?

3.6    During the time of marital disintegration,
       did you and your spouse ever switch roles

as the active and passive agents? If so, how did this happen?

**3.7** Evaluate this statement: "Couples in the midst of breaking up rarely understand what divorce does to the people who are ·involved" (p. 52).

## Chapter Four: The Ripping Apart of One Flesh

**4.1** In Genesis 2 God says marriage partners become "glued" together in a one-flesh relationship. A popular term today is *codependence*. This could be defined as "being in an unhealthy 'glued' relationship." On the other hand, a healthy relationship could be described as *interdependent* (p. 54).

What might be some positive aspects of being "glued" to someone (interdependence)?

What might be some negative aspects of being "glued" to someone (codependence)?

4.2    How have you experienced the ambiva-
       lence found in a broken one-flesh relation-
       ship?


4.3    Pages 55–57 describe the way separation
       and divorce disrupt almost every area of
       life.

       Remember the "Before and After" page
       you started at the beginning of these
       study questions? Review this sheet now
       and jot down any areas you have not
       thought of up to this point.


       How has your divorce disrupt your life?

       How has your divorce disrupted your life?

4.4    Have you felt social rejection as a result of
       your divorce? If so, give several examples.


4.5    What do you think of the idea that pain is
       a natural result of breaking the relation-
       ship contract of marriage (pp. 60–61)?

4.6    Respond to this comment: "Running from
       the pain [of divorce] will only prolong its
       impact" (p. 62).


       How have you run from the pain of di-
       vorce?


4.7    List some benefits that can be gained by
       facing and dealing with the hurt of di-
       vorce rather than running from it (p. 62).


4.8    We usually think of grief and mourning
       only in the context of death. What do you
       think of the idea that you must go through
       grief and mourning in the loss of your
       marriage (p. 63)?


4.9    What understanding of the stages of
       grieving (p. 64) did you have before read-
       ing this book?

4.10   Pages 64–65 describe the slippery slope. You may want to refer to this section as you read the next chapters.

## Chapter Five: Putting Off Until Tomorrow What I Don't Want Today (The Experience of Denial)

5.1   Here are some of the phrases used in this chapter to define *denial:*

- A response used "when we don't want to face a fact or circumstance" (p. 67).
- "A reaction to circumstances that are beyond one's control" (p. 68).
- "An attempt to isolate oneself against reality and all of the pain that is taking place" (p. 68).
- "Putting up a facade . . . a fantasy world where things are so much better than what they really are in your life" (p. 71).
- "A quick way of regaining emotional equilibrium" (p. 71).

Do any of these phrases ring true to your experience? Why?

How have you experienced denial during your separation/divorce? Try to write at least three specific instances and occurrences in which you have experienced it.

What are some ways you have observed other people using denial?

5.2 When do you think the use of denial becomes a hindrance to a person?

When do you think it would be healthy for a person to use denial?

5.3 Write down the thoughts that come to your mind when you read this verse from the Bible: "You can't heal a wound by saying it's not there!" (Jer. 6:14 TLB).

5.4 Excluding your separation and divorce, describe three crises you have faced in your life.

1. _____

2. _____

3. _____

How did the use of denial help you during these times?

5.5   How would you evaluate your use of denial during your separation and divorce?

5.6   What are some of the unpleasant realities of separation and divorce that you have not been willing to face?

5.7   One of the major reasons people stay in denial is fear.

      What fears has marital breakup created in you?

What changes are you being forced to handle?

5.8   At the end of this chapter John comments, "Those were the two things that helped me the most: time and others who understood what I was going through" (p. 76).

How long have you been separated? _____

How long have you been divorced? _____

How long do you think it should take for someone to stop retreating from the shock of a marital breakup?

Why?

## Chapter Six: The Volcano Within (Anger)

6.1   On pages 78–79 the author shares ways people express the anger of divorce. If you were asked to illustrate the anger of divorce from your own experience, what story or stories would you tell?

Why do you believe the anger of divorce can be so prolonged and intense?

6.2    The anger of divorce can take many active and passive forms. Note the following, taken from page 78. See if you can add at least three more to each list.

| Active Forms of Anger | Passive Forms of Anger |
|---|---|
| sarcasm | stubbornness |
| criticism | restlessness |
| impatience | self-pity |
| cruelty | withdrawal |

Do you find yourself using more active or passive forms of anger?

6.3    Page 79 refers to a study showing that close to 80 percent of anger is a response to the actions of others. This study concludes that anger is a relationship response. Do you agree or disagree with this conclusion? Why?

6.4    "When it comes to the anger of divorce, the feelings can be as intense as the intimacy that once characterized the marriage" (p. 80). In what ways has your experience proved this statement?

6.5    How were you trained to view anger when you were growing up? Review the following statements and check those that best state the attitude of your childhood family toward anger. Feel free to add any additional or alternative phrases.

_____ 1. "Don't you dare get angry at me."
_____ 2. "It isn't right for us to get angry."
_____ 3. "I know you are angry, Honey. What is happening to make you feel this way?"
_____ 4. "We all get angry, but the way you are using your anger is wrong."
_____ 5. "Go to your room!"

Your own statements:

_____ 6. _____

_____ 7. _____

Recall one instance when you were angry or hurt as a child. Take a piece of paper and write your memories of that incident.

6.6    On page 81 the author makes a distinction
       between anger feelings and anger man-
       agement. Perhaps this is the first time you
       have come across the difference between
       feelings and the management of those
       feelings. Take a moment and write defini-
       tions of these two concepts.

       *Anger feelings* are:


       *Anger management* is:



6.7    The following work sheet is to be used in
       conjunction with the discussion of anger
       management found on pages 82–90. Fill in
       the following questions, using the infor-
       mation found on these pages and your ex-
       perience.

       **The Four Methods of Anger Management**

       **Rage**

       *Rage* can be defined as:


       Ways I have seen others use rage are:

Ways I have used rage are:

The results of rage are:

## Repression

*Repression* can be defined as:

Ways I have seen others use repression are:

Ways I have used repression are:

The results of repression are:

## Resolution

*Resolution* can be defined as:

Ways I have seen others use resolution are:

Ways I have used resolution are:

The results of resolution are:

**Redirection**

*Redirection* can be defined as:

Ways I have seen others use redirection are:

Ways I have used redirection are:

The results of redirection are:

6.8    Using anger in a constructive way is a tremendous challenge (p. 90). List three ways a proper use of anger could change or improve your life.

   1.

2.


3.


## Chapter Seven: Microwave Solutions to Crockpot Problems (Bargaining)

7.1    What are some bargains you and your former spouse have used during your separation/divorce? List three or more below.

1.


2.


3.


7.2    Discuss how in your divorce you have protected or defended yourself through bargaining.

How has your bargaining reflected your priorities or major concerns?

7.3   The author makes a distinction between bargaining and negotiation. Using the information on pages 93–95, write your own definitions of these two terms.

*Bargaining* is:

*Negotiation* is:

7.4   Many see bargaining as selfish manipulation or a power play (pp. 94–95). How have you felt when a bargaining ploy has been pulled on you?

7.5   Now suppose you try the bargaining game on someone else and it works. In the midst of getting what you want, how have you treated the other person involved?

7.6   It is easy to be impatient. We look for
      quick and easy solutions to resolve our
      complex problems (p. 96). What areas
      challenged your patience most during
      your separation and divorce?

7.7   Reread the story of Mike and Doris
      Bridges on pages 96–97. Note these two
      key sentences on page 97:

      • "They make promises and state their ex-
        pectations, but Mike never demon-
        strated behavioral changes to validate
        any hope for a difference in their mar-
        riage."
      • "Without hard work and life-style
        changes, all the hope in the world
        would not resolve their difficulties."

      When have you been led to believe some-
      one, only to be disappointed?

7.8   The story of John Peters (pp. 98–99)
      teaches that some of us learned to use bar-
      gaining in our families when we were
      growing up. As you reflect on your child-
      hood, how might you have learned to use
      manipulative power plays to get what you
      want?

7.9    To help us break the bargaining habit, the
       author proposes a number of questions on
       pages 99–100 about our attitudes toward
       others.

       Select two or more significant others in
       your life, persons with whom you have
       had disagreements or conflicts. The first
       is your former spouse. The second is your
       choice. Write their names below:

       1. Former spouse: _____

       2. Other:            _____

       Considering one person at a time, respond
       to the following questions:

       • How do I feel toward this person?


       • Am I trying to get my own way, or am I
         sincerely interested in coming to a joint
         conclusion?



7.10   It is tough not to play the bargaining
       game. Sometimes we need encourage-
       ment and support as we work to break old
       habits (p. 100). Who is one person with
       whom you could share the ideas in this
       chapter and who could support you in
       learning not to play this game?

## Chapter Eight: How Low Can
## I Go? (Depression)

8.1   Periods of depression are a normal part of
      the recovery process (p. 104). What are
      some ways you have experienced depres-
      sion during your separation and divorce?

8.2   While in recovery we must understand
      that factors other than our marital dis-
      ruption should be considered when facing
      depression (p. 104). Are any of the follow-
      ing adding stress to your experience of di-
      vorce? Check the appropriate responses.

| **Physical Condition** | **Yes** | **Maybe** | **No** |
| --- | --- | --- | --- |
| Poor exercise habits | | | |
| Unbalanced nutrition | | | |
| Lack of sleep | | | |
| Excess sleep | | | |
| Chronic illness | | | |
| Vitamin or mineral deficiency | | | |
| Flu or cold symptoms | | | |
| Prolonged illness or convalescence | | | |
| Multiple prescription drugs | | | |
| Overeating | | | |
| Heavy drinking of alcohol | | | |
| Heavy smoking | | | |
| Bodily injury | | | |

Physical abuse
Loss or gain of fifteen or more
   pounds

| **Emotional Condition** | Yes | Maybe | No |
|---|---|---|---|

Critical self-talk
Dysfunctional family background
Emotional abuse
Past physical or emotional trauma
Past emotional struggles
Adult-child issues
Previous divorce experiences
Codependency struggles
Compulsive behaviors
Unresolved bitterness or anger
Guilt
Shame
Areas of embarrassment
Emotional outbursts
Discomfort if not busy

| **Spiritual Condition** | Yes | Maybe | No |
|---|---|---|---|

Uncertain of relationship with God
Lack assurance of salvation
Feel you must be better for God
Feel God dislikes you
Little or no prayer
Little or no meditation on God's
   truth
Aversion to fellowship

Not involved in small group
Self-focused and not giving to others
Little or no worship with others
Little or no private worship
No time to work on inner world
Do not enjoy being by myself

These lists are not exhaustive, but they help give you a sense of how you are doing in each area of life.

If you checked three or more yes statements in a single category, consider the following about that category.

**Physical**

When was the last time you had a complete physical examination?


If it has been over a year, it might be helpful to have one during this time of added stress.

**Emotional**

Have you ever been or are you currently in counseling?


If not, it might be helpful to sit down for an hour with a counselor and discuss your current experiences. An objective perspective on your circumstances could be a real lift!

If you have been in counseling before, think about sharing your current experiences with that person.

### Spiritual

Many of us become so busy or involved in our current experiences that we disregard the spiritual area of life. You might find it encouraging to talk with a pastor about the things you checked on this list. If you don't have a pastor, feel free to call the Fresh Start office at 1-800-882-2799 for a referral.

8.3     Pages 104–107 outline characteristics of divorce depression. Read the description of each characteristic and consider the questions for that area.

### Sadness: low in spirit, hopeless, and helpless

How have you felt sad during separation/ divorce?


What are triggers to sadness, things that

cause you to move into a sad state of mind?

### Loneliness and withdrawal: pulling away from people, ceasing to trust others

How have you experienced withdrawal from others?

What are triggers to withdrawal, things that cause you to pull away from others?

### Pessimistic attitude: applying the negative consequences of divorce to every aspect of life

Before your marital disruption do you think people would have considered you a pessimistic person? Explain your answer.

What are ways you have thought and acted in a pessimistic manner during your separation/divorce?

What are triggers to pessimism, things that cause you to feel pessimistic?


## Not paying attention to personal health and appearance

What are ways your health and/or appearance has changed during your separation/divorce?


How have these changes made you feel about yourself?


## Neglecting enjoyable activities

What are activities, projects, or hobbies you have enjoyed? (Don't restrict your response to your married, or just your adult, life. Think back even to your childhood—what did you like to do?)


When was the last time you had fun?


What is preventing you from participating

in an enjoyable activity within the next week?

8.4     The author states that depression is not necessarily a sign of personal or spiritual weakness. Great saints of the Bible experienced it. Depression can act as a God-given circuit breaker to protect our emotional system (pp. 108–109).

How do you respond to this perspective on depression?

Compare this view of depression with how you feel about yourself.

8.5     A recently separated friend asked, "How could God let me go through this?" Yet on pages 109–10 the author states it is important to affirm God's control in your separation and divorce.

How have you struggled in believing that a good God could allow separation and divorce in your life?

8.6    On page 110 the author refers to the story
       of Joseph in the Bible (Gen. 37; 39—50).
       Take about fifteen minutes and read this
       story. Notice the pain, injustice, and diffi-
       culty Joseph experienced.

       What significance did believing in God's
       control have for Joseph while he was go-
       ing through his difficulties?

8.7    How might serving others help you deal
       with the depression of divorce (pp. 111–
       13)?

       Outside your daily routine, what are two
       ways you could take Menninger's advice
       to "find someone in need, and do some-
       thing to help that person" (p. 112)?

8.8    One way to deal with divorce depression is
       to evaluate how you feel about yourself
       (p. 113). The following exercises, adapted
       from *The Adult Child of Divorce* (Bob
       Burns and Michael J. Brissett, Jr., Oliver-
       Nelson, 1991, pp. 176-77), will help you re-
       view your thought patterns.

Our self-talk both reflects and determines the beliefs we hold. It also affects the way we feel. What we say to ourselves—and what we hear others repeat—we often believe as truth. The following list includes statements you might be repeating to yourself. Read the list and fill in the blanks. Then put a check beside any of these statements you think you say to yourself repeatedly.

As a person going through separation and divorce, I may be saying to myself that:

My value is _____

I am valuable when _____

My security is _____

I am secure when _____

My worst faults are _____

My best qualities are _____

I worry about _____

I am responsible for _____

I feel guilty when _____

It would be wonderful if _____

It would be awful if _____

I must _____

I cannot _____

Safety is _____

My body is _____

Others are trustworthy when _____

Danger is when _____

Success is when _____

Others are reliable when _____

Evil in the world is _____

For me to get angry is _____

For me to show hurt is _____

For me to show fear is _____

I am most looking forward to _____

I will be happy when _____

Others think I am _____

Other messages I seem to repeat to myself include:

1. _____

2. _____

3. _____

4. _____

5. _____

8.8     Forgiveness is tough work. It can be hard
        to forgive others. It can be doubly hard to
        forgive yourself (p. 113).

        Can you list three things for which it is
        hard to forgive yourself?

        1.


        2.


        3.



8.9     On page 114 the author suggests that, to
        deal with divorce depression, you should
        find others who will listen and under-
        stand what you are experiencing. Refer to
        question 5.8 for specific suggestions on
        how you can seek out people with whom
        you can talk.


8.10    Many people are surprised to learn that
        reaching depression means you are mov-
        ing closer to acceptance (p. 115). How do
        you respond to this statement?

## Chapter 9: Redefining Normal
## (Acceptance)

9.1   If you really made it to full acceptance,
      what do you think life would be like?

9.2   Many of us have a fantasized idea of ac-
      ceptance. Reread pages 118–20 to develop
      your own definitions of *acceptance* and
      *resignation*.

      *Resignation* is:

      *Acceptance* is:

      Compare these two concepts, jotting
      down similarities and differences be-
      tween them.

9.3   Many people confuse the stage of accep-
      tance with the idea that they have ac-
      cepted the fact of their divorce (p. 121).

      What is the difference between under-
      standing the fact of divorce and coming to
      acceptance?

How might you have confused them in your experience?

9.4   Use the following work sheet to process your understanding of the six characteristics of acceptance. Some of the information for this work sheet is given on pages 122–35; other responses must come from your meditation and experience, as well as the experiences of others.

| Characteristic | Action Steps Needed to Put This into Practice | How I Am Doing in This Area |
|---|---|---|
| 1. Recognizing your marriage is over and your divorce is complete | | |
| 2. Being honest with yourself and your feelings | | |
| 3. Establishing and maintaining friendships | | |
| 4. Learning to control your thought life | | |
| 5. Looking forward, not backward | | |
| 6. Developing a new source of hope | | |

9.5     Each of us has a belief system (p. 134). If someone were to ask you, "What are your beliefs about life, about God, and about hope?" how would you respond?

During separation and divorce the strength and validity of our beliefs are tested (p. 134). We are forced to examine what we really believe and depend on. How has this happened to you?

If you were to die tonight and God asked you, "Why should I let you into My heaven?" what would you say?

## Chapter Ten: How Does God Feel About Me?

10.1    On page 138 the author states, "There is no pain that strikes the core of the soul like the rejection of a friend." How have you experienced rejection by a friend?

What would it take for you to be reconciled to that friend again?

10.2 After reading Pam's story (pp. 139–43), decide what it would take for you to be reconciled with your former spouse (if, indeed, a reconciliation could actually take place).

10.3 How do you respond to the idea that God has taken the initiative to be reconciled to you (pp. 143–50)?

10.4 How can you know if you have been forgiven and accepted by God (pp. 150–51)?

10.5 Knowing God is different from simply being religious (pp. 155–57). How would you describe this difference?

If the idea of knowing God and being a Christian is confusing to you, feel free to call Fresh Start at 1-800-882-2799. We would be happy to talk with you about it.

## *In Conclusion*

After reading this book, name one chapter you
would describe as absolutely essential reading
for someone else.